BRITISH SALOON CARS
OF THE
FIFTIES

First published 1985 by Haynes Publishing Group

This edition published 1995 by The Promotional
Reprint Company Ltd, exclusively for
Bookmart Limited, Desford Road, Enderby,
Leicester LE9 5AD

ISBN 1 85648 255 3

Printed and bound in China

BRITISH SALOON CARS
OF THE
FIFTIES

MICHAEL ALLEN

Credits

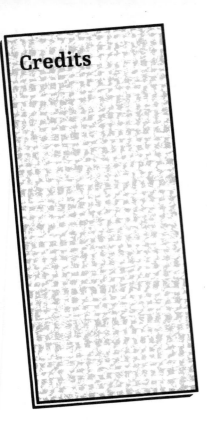

Whilst researching for this book I did of course have to check facts, and I am particularly grateful to Howard Foottit who lent me much of his collection of old motoring literature, Steve Waldenberg for information in respect of the sidevalve engined Fords, Barry Findlaw who also provided me with information, particularly in respect of certain Vauxhall models, and John Barker for details of the Austin A70s. Thanks are also due to Ray Hutton of *Autocar* and John Thorpe of *Motor* for their permission to use performance figures from their respective magazines.

Several of the photographs used in the Ford chapter came from Ford Photographic Services, and for these my thanks go to Steve Clark and Sheila Knapman. Obtaining photographs from other manufacturers however proved difficult to say the least, and in fact several alternative sources had to be found. Fortunately, many enthusiasts willingly came to my assistance here, and I am therefore very grateful to the following who supplied me with much material from which to choose: Dave Turner, Nigel Palethorpe, Geoffrey Greenwood, R. A. Dyson, Neil Tee, Colin Moorhouse, Simon Walker, Gordon Love, Bob Cleversley, John Billinger, D. J. Garrett, Robert Bovey, David Williams, Ken Hobday, Tony Gilroy, Ray Newell, Howard Foottit, John Barker, Barry Findlaw, Phil Ansell, Kim Henson and Melvyn Smith.

Michael G. D. Allen

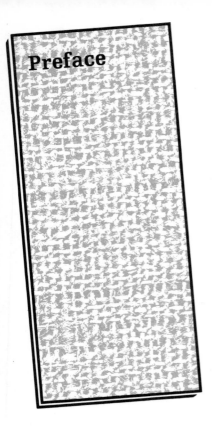

Any passenger car with room for four or more people can be said to be a 'family' model; therefore, such as the Rover P4 series, the Humber Hawks and Super Snipes, Jaguar saloons, Rileys, Wolseleys etc., and even a Rolls-Royce in fact, could all claim to be family cars. However, cars bearing these, and similarly prestigious names, in the 1950s were always aimed up-market to a greater or lesser degree, and, although badge engineering was taking place by then, even relatively inexpensive models such as the Wolseley 1500, or a Singer Gazelle were certainly not considered 'ordinary' by most people. This was largely because, unlike the situation today, the once relatively exclusive marque names which had been absorbed into larger car manufacturing groups were still reserved for the group's up-market-image models only, in which a genuine effort was made to give the customer a measure of the qualities for which the marque in question was best remembered. So, at a time when it would have been inconceivable to have thought of a Rover badge, for instance, ending up on a thinly disguised mass-market import from the other side of the world, it was the more humble Austins, Fords, Hillmans, etc. which most people thought of as the real family models, and a Rover, MG Magnette, or Sunbeam Rapier, or indeed any of the aforementioned up-market cars were thought of as a genuine luxurious/sporting businessman's saloon rather than a family workhorse.

It is for these reasons that in this book I have not included the rather more exclusive passenger cars, even those sharing some components with much cheaper mass-market models. Instead I have concentrated on the cars which, whilst often proving to be excellent products, were nevertheless quite unashamedly down-market in that at all levels they were attempting to widen the motoring scene rather than appeal to the more selective buyer who perhaps valued a measure of exclusivity for its own sake. My own interest in the ordinary cars of the 'fifties stems from the Sunday outings of the early 1950s of which I have a vivid recall. By that time, new postwar Austin, Ford, Hillman, Morris, Standard, and Vauxhall models at the lower end of the market could all be seen in addition to the large number of old-fashioned pre-war cars still giving yeoman service. Living in Leeds, we were well placed for visiting both the east and west coast resorts, although with four of us in my father's 'upright' Anglia a trip to either coast could be a 2½ hour affair even without delays at such bottlenecks as Malton, on the way to Scarborough. Between York and Bridlington was the notorious Garrowby Hill, and if the little Ford was baulked here by a well-laden pre-war '8', or even a '7' (there were still plenty of those about) then a quick double-de-clutch would be necessary to avoid coming to rest, and we would grind over the summit in first gear. How we envied those new Zephyrs as they effortlessly floated past on the climb – still in top gear! A second-hand Morris Oxford MO series replaced the Anglia in 1953, giving us a whole new level of comfort and knocking half-an-hour or so off the journey times to the coast on a good run, whilst in 1956 a brand-new Mk2 Consul brought the seaside nearer still.

A trip to these resorts 25 or 30 years ago would usually see the promenade literally crawling with such as Austin Somersets, Hillman Minxes, Consuls, Minors, Standard Eights etc., and mingling amongst these would be the Vanguards, Zephyrs, Veloxes and Westminsters: these last three models having at last brought the refinements of six-cylinder motoring within the reach of a large number of people.

Certainly, there are a great many people in Britain today who look back with real affection at their Morris Oxford, Vauxhall Wyvern or similarly inexpensive model from the 1950s, remembering these cars for the happy countryside picnics and seaside trips on summer Sundays, but also for their honest-to-goodness integrity which was characterized by the very lack of today's "high-tech" features such as digital displays and synthesized voices; not to mention computerized engine management systems and underbonnet layouts which now render the once simple Saturday morning tune-up in the driveway a thing of the past. True enough, now, a three-speed column change gearbox with an unsynchronized first gear, and vacuum operated windscreen wipers do seem somewhat vintage if not exactly pre-historic. Nevertheless, there's many an elderly driver today who will tell you in all sincerity that his old Consul or Zephyr was "the best car I ever had", whilst someone else will lovingly recall how their little Austin A30, with a roof-rack piled high "never missed a beat" during a 400 mile round trip on the annual summer holiday.

Similar nostalgic claims can be heard today in respect of all the "bread and butter" cars of 30 years ago, and there is no doubt that this affection was generated because these cars so often did at least as much as, and sometimes much more than, some expensive cars could do, and whilst nostalgia is playing a part in the present-day interest in these cars there is also recognition amongst younger enthusiasts that despite the lack of a walnut facia and a high price tag, these cars are well worth restoring to their former glory in which condition they can give excellent service once again whilst providing transport that is certainly different from today's norm, but still at prices well within reach. I hope therefore that this book will appeal to both those who simply wish to take a nostalgic look once more at their past pride and joy; and perhaps compare its features once again with those of its contemporaries in those far off days, and to the new owners who are now playing such an active part in the 1950s revival which is happening in Britain today – a motoring revival in which I have most certainly enjoyed participating in recent years.

Michael Allen

Chapter 1

The Early Development of the Family Car in Britain

The 'family' car, so-called because of its ability to carry at the very least, mother, father, and two children, at an overall cost of operation appreciably less than that of the more highly priced genuine luxury saloons, owes its very existence to the late Henry Ford.

"I will build a car for the great multitude" Ford once said, and, after several abortive attempts, he did just that with the introduction in 1908 of his immortal Model T, at a time when the other infant motor manufacturers were concentrating on the development of well-appointed carriages aimed at the wealthy minorities. The secret of the Model T's success was its simplicity and the resultant ease with which it could be built, these factors enabling Ford to improve production methods constantly, and then reduce the price of the car with each advance in manufacturing technique.

Inevitably, other manufacturers began to follow Ford's lead, and indeed, despite some periodic updating in styling features, when the Model T finally came to the end of its incredible 19 year production run, during which time some 15,000,000 examples had taken to the road, it was thoroughly outdated by comparison with the later products of rival manufacturers who were now aiming at the same expanding market.

Production of the Model T came to Britain in 1911, with the formation of the Ford Motor Company (England) Ltd., and only two years later, the company's Trafford Park, Manchester, plant was Europe's largest car producer. In 1914, the moving assembly line technique which Ford had so successfully pioneered at Highland Park, Detroit, was introduced to Trafford Park, Manchester, and for

1911 and mass-production comes to Britain in the form of Henry's Model T, built at Trafford Park. As the plaque shows, the buyer could be on the road for £116. 12s. 8d and two-hours of driving instruction was deemed sufficient – no L-test in those days! (Courtesy National Motor Museum, Beaulieu).

the time being at least, the Model T tightened its grip on the British market.

Of the early British pioneers, the one most impressed by Ford's methods was Oxford-based William Morris, who, accompanied by one of his engineers, twice journeyed to Detroit in order to see for himself the successful American auto industry at work. Morris' first car, introduced in 1913, and appropriately named "Oxford", was somewhat limited in its sales appeal as it was a strict two-seater, but his next model, the famous "Bullnose" Cowley, was to be available in both two and four seat form.

The first World War now intervened, and it was not until 1919 that the Ford versus Morris battle for supremacy in Britain really got underway. In the early postwar boom, Ford took the lead, with the Model T accounting for over 40% of all new car sales in Britain in 1919. However, this lead was to be short lived. The principal reason for the Ford's success was without doubt its low first cost, the £220 price tag comfortably undercutting the £330 being asked for the Morris Cowley, but with the introduction in 1921 of the "horsepower" annual road tax, the picture changed considerably. This tax, which was calculated on the engine's bore size rather than its total capacity, was heavily biased against the large bore Ford engine. The owner of a Model T would now have to pay a £22 yearly tax, whereas the narrow-bored engine in the Morris Cowley was attracting only a £12 annual duty. Ford sales in Britain quickly began to fall, and by 1925 Morris had taken over as the biggest selling make.

The products of Britain's other well-known early pioneer, Herbert Austin, had not yet made a really significant impact on the family car market, but the diminutive Austin Seven, introduced in 1922 in answer to the horsepower tax, was quickly establishing a firm following. The Austin Seven incorporated many of the desirable features of much larger models, but in a scaled down form, and was thus the first successful attempt at producing a very small "real" car. A year after its introduction, the capacity of the engine was raised slightly, from 700 to 750cc, and continued development of the model was to keep it in production, and extremely competitive, right through to 1939 by which time almost, 300,000 examples had left the Longbridge factory. In 1929, in an obvious effort to capture some of the Austin Seven's market, Morris introduced the similarly sized Minor. At first powered by an overhead camshaft engine which was based on a Wolseley design, Morris having added the ailing Wolseley Company to his growing empire some time previously, the Minor proved to be too sophisticated for the economy end of the market. In 1931 a simple sidevalve engine replaced the ohc unit, but even in this form the Minor failed to make a really serious challenge to the well established "baby" Austin.

Meanwhile, the fortunes of the Ford Motor Company had sunk to an all time low in Britain. The Model T had been discontinued in 1927, after which Henry Ford had started his "alphabet" series all over again with the introduction of a completely new and thoroughly up to date Model A. In view of the horsepower tax in Britain, a small-bored version of the new Ford, the Model AF, took over at Trafford Park, with plans to eventually switch production to the company's new purpose-built plant which was rapidly taking shape by the side of the river Thames at Dagenham. However, by the time production commenced at Dagenham, in October 1931, the Model AF was already a failure in Britain. Despite the 14hp rating of its narrow-bored engine, the British motoring public had never taken to the AF in anything like sufficient numbers, and it was becoming clear that if the amazing mass production facilities at Dagenham were to be utilised to the full, a small economical Ford, designed in its entirety specifically for the needs of Britain and Europe would be needed quickly.

The parent company acted very quickly indeed, and in August 1932 Dagenham was able to offer the British public the first 8 horsepower Ford, the Model Y. The heart of the Model Y was a robust 4 cylinder engine of 933cc, its power being transmitted to the rear axle by a three-speed gearbox complete with synchromesh between the two upper ratios, a specification which gave a 60mph, or 40mpg capability according to choice. The slightly raked back radiator and windscreen, coupled with a flowing mudguard design gave the little Ford an elegance not before seen in a really small car, and with its asking price of £120 undercutting both the Austin Seven and the Morris Minor, its sales success was assured.

Morris countered the model Y in the quickest possible way, by simply purchasing a new Ford, stripping it down, and then producing a remarkably similar car announced in 1934 as the new Morris 8. Offering almost exactly the same performance and accomodation as the Ford, the new Morris was equipped with rather more sophisticated running gear, including hydraulic brakes, and a four door saloon with leather upholstery represented good value in 1934 at £142.

Dagenham's answer was a series of price cuts, bringing the Model Y down to £115, then £110, and finally in October 1935 to just £100, the only time a full four-seater production saloon has ever been offered at this magic figure. By this time, Ford enthusiasts also had the choice of a 10 horsepower car; the rather barrel-shaped Model C, powered by the now legendary 1172cc sidevalve engine, had been added to the Ford range the year before. Between them, the Models Y and C took a share of the small car market in Britain which Ford have held onto ever since.

Although Morris, Austin, and Ford were by this time established as the "Big Three' in Britain, other manufacturers were also offering some excellent inexpensive saloons for the family motorist. The Standard Motor Company made a strong challenge in 1935 with the introduction of the "Flying" Standard range: 9 and 12 horsepower models in which smooth styling was a very prominent feature. The Rootes Group were offering the 10 horsepower Hillman Minx, and Vauxhall, after being rescued in 1925 by the other American giant, General Motors, were also making headway in this important market sector, their 1938 10/4 model being particularly

A well-used 1939 Vauxhall 10/4 two-door saloon. With the backing of General Motors, Vauxhall were strong enough to enter the fray in the middleweight family car division with this model. The 10/4 was also significant for being the first British car built on monocoque principles. (Courtesy National Motor Museum, Beaulieu).

noteworthy inasmuch that it featured monocoque construction for the first time on a British car.

When the war-clouds which had once again gathered over Europe finally burst, passenger car production was inevitably replaced by the manufacture of more warlike equipment. Virtually any hardware needed with which to wage war, from steel helmets to four-engined bombers, was turned out by the car manufacturers over the next five years or so before hostilities ceased.

Naturally enough, the early crop of postwar cars were the already-familiar models from the late 1930s, quickly re-introduced with barely any revision in order to satisfy the immediate demand, whilst giving the development engineers some time in which to come up with new postwar designs which would be more appropriate in the rapidly changing world. Exporting was now of prime importance, and the British car manufacturers had to take more seriously than ever before the widely varying demands of overseas markets. As a result of these considerations, there began to emerge in the late 1940s the first of what was to be a steady stream of new inexpensive family models, many of which displayed considerable advances over their 1930s predecessors.

All steel monocoque construction offered many advantages in the medium size of car which had the widest export appeal. An extremely rigid bodyshell, which would stand up well to colonial conditions was possible with this method of construction, which also gave a worthwhile saving in weight which in turn had a beneficial effect on both performance and fuel economy. These latter benefits were further enhanced by the increasing use of overhead-valve engines which developed more power from a given capacity than did the then traditional sidevalve units. Independent front suspension systems, and hydraulic brakes all-round gave new levels of roadworthiness in keeping with the increase in performance.

That these cars were successful, is of course now well known. Throughout the 1950s, British cars earned an enviable reputation in foreign markets, and in Britain today an ever growing number of car enthusiasts look upon the 1950s as the period which produced the best-ever crop of "ordinary" family cars. In the pages which follow we will take a close look at these successful ordinary cars – The Fifties Family Cars – from the British Motor Manufacturers.

The Austin Motor Company entered the 1950s with one of the most notable of the early postwar successes to their credit. The A40 Devon (4 door) and Dorset (2 door), introduced in late 1947 had gained world wide approval, including that of America, to such an extent that the model had established itself as Britain's biggest dollar earning car up to that time.

Of quite conventional design, the A40 featured a separate chassis frame of longitudinal box section members with transverse members front and rear. Further bracing was provided by elongated X-bracing with shorter transverse stiffeners from the X-frame to the outer main chassis rails. Bolted to this chassis was roomy bodywork which, in four door form, was of six light window design. Flowing wing lines – with built in headlamps at the front – and the lack of

You see more Austins on the roads of Britain today than any other single make of car

The A40 — today's champion dollar earner for Britain.

AUSTINS LAST LONGER

How do old Austins spend their old age? By continuing to pay their way with vigorous, trouble-free performance on the roads. They may have made their debut as long ago as '35, '33 or even '32, but they still persist in keeping up with younger cars — and often pass them. These old Austins wear so well because they are made so well; and, like them, the new A40 is built to give dependable service first — and last.

This 1933 Austin 'Ten' is still on very active service.

AUSTIN—you can depend on it!

THE AUSTIN MOTOR CO LTD · LONGBRIDGE · BIRMINGHAM

A 1949 advertisement depicting the dollar-earning A40, and also pointing out that many much older Austins were still going strong.

running boards were up-to-date features which gave the A40 a modern appearance. A useful feature of this bodywork was the rear-hinged deep-sided bonnet which gave excellent side access for routine maintenance. At the rear was a rather small luggage boot, this did however have the benefit of a drop-down lid with hinges sufficiently strong to allow the lid to be used as a platform in exceptional circumstances. The spare wheel was housed in the luggage compartment beneath a false floor.

The passenger doors were front hinged in the modern manner, and the A40's interior was finished to quite high standards for what was a relatively inexpensive car. Standard equipment included window winding mechanism in the doors, with the addition of swivelling quarter windows for 1950, twin sunvisors, comprehensive instrumentation, and a sprung three spoke steering wheel. A steel sliding sunroof was available at extra cost, as was a heater unit.

The engine was a new pushrod-operated-ohv unit of 1200cc. With its single carburettor, and a compression ratio of 7.2:1, this engine developed 40bhp at 4200rpm. A four-speed gearbox featured synchromesh between the three upper ratios, these being selected by means of a long floor-mounted lever. The lever was arranged so that, when in the third and top gear plane, it came conveniently close to the steering wheel rim; thus making the change between the two upper ratios a quick and simple matter for main road overtaking. A rear axle ratio of 5.14:1 gave overall gearing of 14.6mph/1000rpm. Coil spring independent front suspension, semi-elliptic leaf springs at the rear, Burman steering gear, Girling brakes of which the front shoes were activated hydraulically and those at the rear by mechanical means, and 16 inch diameter road wheels with 5.25 section tyres completed a then quite up-to-date specification.

Despite compact dimensions – 12 feet 9 inches long and 5 feet 1 inch wide – the A40 weighed in at just over 19cwt. Nevertheless, the 1200cc engine would accelerate the car to 60mph in around 45 seconds, and on to a maximum of more than 65mph under favourable

The A70 Hereford replaced the Hampshire in October 1950. Performance characteristics were similar to the preceding model. This contemporary advertisement shows how patriotism was a feature of Austin's hard sale technique.

The imposing appearance of the A70 Hampshire is captured well in these recent views of a beautifully restored example.

16

The A40 Somerset took over from the Devon in 1952, and continued to sell well. As this contemporary advertisement shows, Austin were very proud of their export successes – and rightly so.

conditions. This was accompanied by an overall fuel consumption of around 30mpg, and at its tax paid price of £501 12s 3d (to which £3 17s 3d had to be added if the sliding roof was specified) the A40 was offering very good value in 1950. Austin's other contender in the family car category at this time was the A70 Hampshire which had been released in mid 1948. The Hampshire was in fact very similar to the A40 from both the structural and styling viewpoint, being built on a larger but otherwise almost identical chassis frame. However, the extra size, and the inclusion of rear wheel spats gave it a sleeker and altogether more impressive appearance, whilst the well-appointed interior could accommodate six people in comfort when required.

The A70's running gear specification was similar to the smaller car, but now of appropriate dimensions to cope with the heavier (25cwt) and much faster model. Under the bonnet was an uprated version of the large four-cylinder ohv engine which had first appeared in 1946 in the Austin Sixteen. With bore and stroke dimensions of 79.4mm x 111mm giving a capacity of 2199cc, and with a single carburettor and a compression ratio of 6.8/1, this engine produced 67bhp at 3800rpm with a useful maximum torque output of 116lbs/ft at 1700rpm. This power was transmitted via a four-speed gearbox to a rear axle with a ratio of 4.125:1 which, in conjunction with 16 inch roadwheels and 5.50 tyres gave usefully high overall gearing of 18.6mph:1000rpm. Translated into performance, these figures meant a full 80mph maximum, an ability to reach 60mph from rest in around 23 seconds, excellent top gear flexibility and an easy 60-65mph cruise. Depending upon the type of use, fuel consumption would be somewhere in the 20-25mpg range. Like the A40, the Hampshire had received front swivelling quarter windows and separate sidelight units for 1950, and at £648, which included a heater as standard, was competitively priced alongside such obvious rivals as the Standard Vanguard (£658), or the 2.2-litre Morris Six at £671.

Rather surprisingly, the Hampshire was destined to have only a short production run, and in October 1950 was replaced by the slightly larger Hereford. Still designated A70, the Hereford was in most respects simply a rebodied Hampshire, being built on the same chassis with only minor differences in the running gear being evident. The wheelbase was increased by 3 inches, achieved by moving the rear spring mountings back by that amount, and the braking system was now all hydraulic.

The lengthened wheelbase allowed the rear seat to be mounted a little further back, thus improving both knee-room and rear compartment access. The latter also benefited from the use of wider rear doors which now resulted in a body of four light design. Once again the interior was well appointed, with the seats being upholstered in leather over Dunlopillo cushions. All four doors were provided with armrests and usefully sized map pockets, and a wide central armrest was a feature of the rear passenger seat. The facia layout included a lidded compartment at each end and a central instrument panel, the centrepiece of which was a circular speedometer which also housed an electric clock. A fuel gauge and ammeter to the left of the speedometer, and gauges for oil-pressure and water temperature to the right completed the instrumentation. Twin horns, operated by a full circle horn ring attached to the sprung steering-wheel, twin sunvisors, a Smiths heating and de-misting unit and swivelling quarter windows in all four doors were standard features of the Hereford's specification. The styling of the car, although considerably updated, still made prominent use of flowing curves. Unfortunately however, the opening section of the bonnet was much smaller than before, and so the Hereford did not offer the excellent underbonnet accessibility of the previous A70.

With the engine output and the overall gearing remaining unchanged the performance and economy levels were also virtually as before, although full use of the well chosen indirect gear ratios was discouraged by the now standard column-change mechanism which, unfortunately, proved to be one of the poorer examples of this type.

Announced simultaneously was an attractive two door convertible by Carbodies of Coventry, and on which a power-operated hood was to be an extra-cost option. An estate car, the A70 Countryman, joined the range during 1951. The Countryman featured wood-framed, steel panelled rear bodywork in which the saloon's curved steel rear wing design was retained.

Meanwhile, the two door A40 Dorset had been discontinued, but the four door Devon continued with only minor revisions; a front bench seat and steering column gearchange having appeared as optional equipment. A new facia was introduced in August 1951 at which time the braking system became all hydraulic, and the column-change appears to have been standardized. It was not until February 1952 that the A40 chassis received an entirely new body which gave it the updated appearance of the larger A70 models. The Somerset, as the new A40 was to be known, was not equipped to the same level as the Hereford, the heater unit and passenger sunvisor being extra-cost

Many cars did, of course, find their way onto the home market, and this well-preserved Somerset – albeit without its overriders – has survived more than 30 years.

options, although leather upholstery was a standard feature. A slight increase in width had provided a little more passenger space, thus making the Somerset unusually roomy for a 1200cc car. The small increase in weight and frontal area were compensated for by the adoption of a modified cylinder-head with larger valves. This head was in fact that being used on the Jensen-bodied A40 Sports which had appeared the previous year.

With 42bhp at 4300rpm and 62lbs/ft torque at 2200rpm, the Somerset in fact proved to be usefully quicker on the road than the Devon, with 70mph just being possible under favourable circumstances. A Somerset convertible followed in August 1952 at which time the larger, and now rather expensive (£1207) Hereford drophead model was deleted. With prices now of £727 for the Somerset, and £976 for the Hereford, these family Austins were not quite so well-placed in their respective classes as had been the earlier A40 and A70, this situation being largely due to more recent developments elsewhere. Nevertheless, they continued to hold their own well, and remained in production until replaced in October 1954 by the new monocoque-bodied Cambridge and Westminster models.

Datapanel: A40 Somerset/A70 Hereford

	A40 Somerset	A70 Hereford
Engine	4 cyl, ohv	4 cyl, ohv
Capacity	1200cc	2199cc
Bore	65.5mm	79.4mm
Stroke	88.9mm	111.1mm
Compression ratio	7.2:1	6.8:1
Max BHP	42 @ 4300rpm	67 @ 3800rpm
Max torque	62lbs/ft @ 2200rpm	116lbs/ft @ 1700rpm
Gearing	14.2mph/1000rpm	18.6mph/1000rpm
Tyres	5.25 x 16	5.50 x 16
Kerb weight	20 1/4cwt	25cwt
Overall length	13ft 3 1/2in	13ft 11 1/2in
Overall width	5ft 3in	5ft 9 1/2in
Wheelbase	7ft 8 1/2in	8ft 3in

Performance

	"The Autocar" Road Tests 1952	"The Autocar" Road Tests 1951
Max speed:		
Top gear	66mph (mean)	80mph (mean)
	71mph (best)	–
3rd gear	49mph	57mph
2nd gear	30mph	34mph
1st gear	20mph	21mph
Acceleration:		
0-30mph	6.9 seconds	5.8 seconds
0-50mph	19.8 seconds	14.9 seconds
0-60mph	36.6 seconds	22.3 seconds
0-70mph	–	36.7 seconds
	Top gear/3rd gear	Top gear/3rd gear
20-40mph	12.9/9.3 seconds	11.2/7.6 seconds
30-50mph	16.5/– seconds	12.1/8.9 seconds
Fuel consumption	28.5mpg (285 miles)	22mpg appprox. overall

Chapter 2
Austin

A30/A35

During the early post war period, the Austin Motor Co. first concentrated on establishing a foothold in the world wide market which existed for medium sized cars, and so it was not until the Earls Court Show of 1951 that the new "Austin Seven" was revealed, the development of which had begun in 1949. In line with the company's post war policy of designating its cars according to the approximate power output of the engine, the new Seven was also to be known as the Austin A30. Unlike on the earlier postwar Austins, the weight saving benefit of monocoque construction had been decided upon for

It's fast! It's economical! It's roomy

'If only Austin would make a Seven again,' people kept saying. 'Nothing could touch it pre-war . . . low-priced, roomy and keeps going for ever.'

Now the new Seven is here. And it's the greatest event in post-war motoring.

Its performance is startling — speed in excess of 60 m.p.h., petrol consumption up to 50 m.p.g. And look at the room . . . the styling . . . the refinements!

Austin's success with high-performance, dependable cars has made the new Seven . . . today's Seven . . . a car that will open the eyes of the world.

● 30 b.h.p. 4-cylinder O.H.V. engine! Independent front suspension! Four rear-opening doors! Ample room for four with luggage!

SPECIFICATION POINTS

Engine : 4-cylinder, overhead valve develops 30 b.h.p. at 4,800 r.p.m.
Clutch : Borg & Beck dry single plate.
Gearbox : Four forward speeds and reverse; synchromesh on 2nd, 3rd and top.
Steering : Special cam gear.
Suspension : Independent coil springs at front; semi-eliptic rear springs. .
Brakes : Full Lockheed hydraulic two leading shoe on front. Hand brake mechanical on rear.
Electrical : 12v battery; provision for interior heating and air circulation; provision for built-in radio.

1951 Motor Show advertisement for the new Austin Seven – shows Austin trying hard to rekindle old, and well-deserved loyalties. Artistic licence in the picture is typical of the period.

Opposite. "Austin of England" is the proud inscription which adorned all Austin A30s and A35s. How times, and attitudes, have changed since the fifties ...

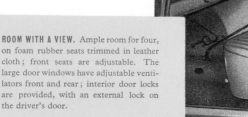

ROOM WITH A VIEW. Ample room for four, on foam rubber seats trimmed in leather cloth; front seats are adjustable. The large door windows have adjustable ventilators front and rear; interior door locks are provided, with an external lock on the driver's door.

this small car, the stressed skin method being used throughout with no chassis type members whatsoever being welded into the lower regions. Careful planning at the design stage also eliminated the need for lead filled joints. Thicker sheet steel than elsewhere was used at strategic points, such as the front suspension mountings; and the result of all this was an extremely light yet adequately sturdy four door bodyshell of compact overall dimensions, which would nevertheless comfortably accommodate four people plus a moderate amount of luggage.

The *NEW* AUSTIN SEVEN

STAND 130

STYLING THAT MAKES SENSE. In the new Seven, Austin achieve a perfect combination of smart appearance, high performance and ample passenger accommodation. The smart lines of the wings are carried on by forward-hinged doors and the streamlined side-lamps are in full view of the driver. The car is 11 feet 4⅚ inches long, 4 feet 7⅛ inches wide and 4 feet 10 inches high; the wheelbase is 6 feet 7½ inches.

GOOD DRIVING MADE EASY. The pleasing, distinctive fascia has everything ready to hand — and eye. It is finished in body colour and has a glove compartment for both driver and passenger. The instruments are well placed and easy to read and under the steering wheel is a finger-tip control for head, side and tail lamps, dipper and horn.

MOST ACCOMMODATING. The capacious rear compartment carries the spare wheel and additionally provides generous luggage room.

AUSTIN

—you can
depend on it!

21

The interior furnishing was very simple, although by careful design successfully managed to avoid a cheap image. The foam rubber seating – individual in the front compartment – was upholstered in pvc, and neatly finished off with piped edges. The felt floor covering was also pvc coated, but in contrast the plain doortrims consisted of nothing more than grained millboard, coloured to match the seats. The instrumentation was limited to a circular speedometer in which was also housed the mileage recorder and a fuel contents gauge. This instrument was positioned centrally in the facia; being flanked on each side by a usefully-sized cubby hole. A heater unit was available as an optional extra, and the provision of a windscreen wiper and sunvisor for the driver only was a rather noticeable economy (similar equipment for the front seat passenger was to become available as an extra cost option). Useful swivelling quarter lights were provided in all four of the forward hinged doors, and the need for window winding mechanism was obviated by providing counterbalanced drop windows in the front doors, whilst the main rear door windows remained fixed.

In the luggage boot, the spare wheel was mounted in an upright position immediately behind the rear seat squab, and with the top of the underslung $5\frac{3}{4}$ gallon capacity fuel tank forming the floor; this compartment was somewhat roomier than the outside appearance suggested. Access was by an almost full width lid with internal spring loaded hinges.

Although aimed very much at the economy end of the market, the new small Austin nevertheless featured chrome plated finish for the bumpers, hubcaps, door handles, lamps, radiator grille, and the traditional "Flying A" bonnet motif. The styling of the car was, however, marred slightly by the use of external door hinges, and the separately mounted sidelamps on the top of the front wings also

Below, left-to-right. A30 four-door, A30 two-door and A35 four-door – spot the differences! Bottom. A30 two-door, pictured from the side, clearly illustrates the distinctive 'Austin-of-the-fifties' look. Certainly the sweeping curves do give an air of elegance to what was after all a very small car.

seemed a little out of place on this otherwise extremely clean and up to date looking model.

A completely new four cylinder engine had been developed for the A30, this unit in fact being the first example of the now famous BMC ''A-series'', which, over thirty years later – in ''A-plus'' form – still powers the BL Metro. Breathing in through a single Zenith carburettor, the new engine for the A30 was of 803cc capacity (58mm bore x 76mm stroke) with a compression ratio of 7.2:1, and featured pushrod-operated overhead valves: a specification which produced 28bhp at 4800rpm and 40lbs/ft torque at 2400rpm. These figures, in conjunction with the car's unladen weight of only a little over 13cwt, promised excellent fuel economy with an entirely acceptable performance level.

The power was transmitted to the rear axle via a hydraulically activated $6\frac{1}{4}$ inch diameter clutch and a four-speed gearbox; the latter, unlike the engine, not being entirely new, having its origins in an earlier Austin 8. Synchromesh was provided between the three upper ratios, the selection of which was by a long floor-mounted lever which was offset from the gearbox centre line; being positioned towards the driver's side. A hypoid rear axle assembly with a ratio of 5.14:1 was employed, giving overall gearing of 12.6mph per 1000rpm on top gear.

The hydraulic braking system – by Lockheed – featured 7 inch diameter drums all round, with a two leading shoe arrangement for the front wheels, and was interesting in that the rear shoes were operated by mechanical links connected to a single rear cylinder mounted ahead of the rear axle, rather than the usual separate wheel cylinder arrangement. The master cylinder itself was situated under the driving compartment floor, from where it was operated directly by the brake pedal.

A beautifully preserved A35 four-door saloon pictured in 1984. Still a very practical and economical car to run, but with real character. Note the surprisingly spacious interior.

The 'Flying-A', chrome grille and Austin motif of the A30 dramatically pictured.

Variations on a theme. The 'Countryman' estate was very popular and offered a great deal of carrying capacity, whilst the Pick-up was only manufactured in small numbers and is rare today. All three of these cars are preserved.

The two independent front suspension units each consisted of a single upper link incorporating the hydraulic shock absorber, a coil spring, and a lower wishbone, with cam and lever steering gear completing the front end arrangements. At the rear, the live axle was located by longitudinally mounted semi-elliptic leaf springs. 13 inch road wheels shod with size 5.20 tyres completed what was then a quite advanced specification for a small economy car, and with its price of £507 undercutting its nearest rival, the four door Morris Minor, by £62, the value for money being offered was impressive.

On the road, the Austin A30 gave a good account of itself, with handling qualities and a general roadworthiness which, whilst not quite up to the standards being set for this class of car by the Morris Minor, were nevertheless of a high order. A maximum speed of

Restored from a derelict hulk in the early eighties, this Speedwell Blue A35 is now powered by a 1275cc Austin-Healey Sprite engine.

62-63mph was accompanied by a rate of acceleration which enabled 50 and 60mph to be reached from rest in around 24 and 39 seconds, whilst fuel consumption figures well in excess of 45mpg were within the reach of those motorists who drove with economy in mind, and even consistently hard driving was unlikely to bring the figure below 40mpg.

Many worthwhile detail improvements to the model were shown at Earls Court in 1953, at which time a two door model – priced at £475 – was also unveiled, thus widening the appeal of this already deservedly popular car. A completely new facia was now introduced, with the centrally mounted instruments now being of an oblong horizontal style. A full width parcel shelf ran beneath the facia panel. The original cloth headlining gave way to one of washable plastic, and new rather less austere door trims also helped to improve the interior scene. A slight redesign of the seating arrangements resulted in 3 inches more knee room for the rear seat passengers, 3 inches more cushion width for those in front, and 2 inches more head-room. On the two door car, the front passenger seat hinged along its front lower edge as well as featuring a hinged squab, an arrangement which made for easy access to the rear compartment. Replacing the internal boot lid hinges with ones mounted externally, moving the spare wheel to a position inside the nearside rear wing, and also moving the petrol filler pipe from its original location through the offside wing to a position low down on the back panel, all combined to give a small but useful increase in luggage space. Externally the A30 now featured twin rear/stop lights, and chromium plated frames for the quarter windows. On the two door car, the rear side windows also featured a chrome plated surround, and were hinged to open outwards from their forward edge. In an effort to improve the fuel economy still further, a new axle ratio of 4.875:1 was adopted early in 1954. The new ratio gave 13.3mph per 1000rpm, and brought figures in excess of 50mpg within the reach of the careful driver. The penalty for this was of course a slight drop in acceleration, which was most noticeable at low speeds in top gear. However, as this was accompanied by a small increase in the actual speed range in each gear, overtaking, particularly in the now rather more useful third gear, was not adversely affected. The absolute maximum speed had now risen to 65-66mph.

Later in 1954, a surprisingly roomy estate car – the A30 Countryman – was added to the range, and attractively priced at £593. The Countryman was based on the recently introduced A30 5cwt van, featuring the same roofline and general rear end appearance apart from the addition of large sliding rear side windows. With the rear seat in its upright position the interior was virtually identical to the saloon, but with the seat squab folded flat, at which its height then matched that of the rear platform, an uninterrupted loading length of 4 feet 5 inches was provided. The full width rear door was hinged on the offside, giving unrestricted access to both the loading area and the spare wheel stowage which was beneath the platform. The unladen weight of the Countryman had risen by more than 1cwt over the saloon, and in view of this plus the anticipated extra loads, an axle ratio of 5.375:1 was employed to lower the overall gearing, although its effect was partly offset by the adoption of larger – 5.60 x 13 – tyres. A slight reduction in performance was of course inevitable, and the maximum speed suffered by some 3 or 4mph, although thanks to the lower gearing the effect on acceleration was hard to detect under about 45mph. The fuel consumption also suffered slightly, but an overall 40mpg was still within reach, a figure which made the A30 Countryman a remarkably economical load carrier.

Although never intended in any way by its manufacturers as a performance car, the A30 did possess a degree of agility which made it competitive enough to score a notable international rally success in May 1956, when a standard two door model was driven to outright victory in the Dutch International Tulip Rally by R. and E. Brookes.

In September 1956, the "Seven" title, which had not in any case been widely used, finally gave way when the designation of the smallest Austin became A35 as a result of the adoption of a larger variation of the A-series engine. Now of 948cc capacity, the unit retained the original cylinder head and valve gear, but utilised a completely new cylinder block with siamezed bores of 63mm diameter. Although the stroke remained the same as before, a new crankshaft with larger diameter main and big end journals was introduced. As in the previous unit, the crankshaft ran in three main bearings, but these and the big end bearings were now of lead indium in place of the more usual white metal. On a compression ratio of 8.3 to 1 the engine's output was now 34bhp at 4500rpm, with a maximum torque figure of 50lbs/ft at 2000rpm. Complementing the improved engine was a new gearbox with more evenly spaced ratios which were now selected by a short floor-mounted remote control gearlever, and a back axle ratio of 4.55:1 which raised the overall gearing to 14.2mph per 1000rpm.

Externally the A35 differed only slightly from the earlier car, being identified from the front by the fact that the radiator grille was now painted, but had a chromium surround, and at the rear by its very usefully enlarged rear window. Separate amber flashing indicators at the front and rear which, unfortunately, were not self cancelling, replaced the semaphore type on the saloon models only, with the Countryman rather curiously continuing to use the earlier arrangement. The range now consisted of basic two and four door models at £541 and £573, with De Luxe versions of these featuring twin windscreen wipers, bumper overriders and, on the two door car, opening rear side windows, priced at £554 and £578. The A35 Countryman, at £638, completed the line up.

A natural outcome of the revised mechanical specification was a totally new level of performance which put the A35 well to the fore for this class of car. Acceleration from rest to 60mph now required only 30 seconds or so, and the maximum speed had risen to rather more than 70mph. The overtaking ability was also much improved, particularly so in the important 30 to 50mph range which could be covered in third gear in 11 seconds. Thanks to the higher overall gearing and the increased efficiency of the higher compression ratio engine, the fuel economy was not impaired under normal driving conditions. Indeed, on a test run made under the scrutiny of the R.A.C., a perfectly standard two door model recorded the remarkable figure of 53.7mpg over a 524 mile route which included both country and city centre running, and which was covered at an average speed of 31.6mph. In a test of a totally different nature, in July 1957, a specially prepared production two door model which

was lightened and "cleaned-up" slightly by the removal of the bumpers, hubcaps, and the protruding sidelamps, captured seven international speed and endurance records for production cars up to 1000cc. This being achieved by lapping the Montlhery racing circuit in France for seven days and nights at an average speed of 74.9mph.

In addition to its obvious appeal as an inexpensive family saloon, in its A35 form the little Austin now possessed characteristics which attracted the more enthusiastic driver. With the increased power available a mild oversteering tendency could be induced with the correct use of the throttle during cornering, particularly if the rear seats were occupied, a situation which gave an almost even front/rear weight distribution, and in skilled hands the A35 was capable of excellent cross country averages over winding roads. Further performance increases were possible if the engine was fitted with one of the variety of tuning conversions available from performance specialists such as Alexander, or Downton engineering. A Downton modified car featuring a reworked cylinder head, twin SU carburettors, and a free flowing exhaust system, could accelerate from 0 to 60mph in 17 seconds and continue to a maximum of around 85mph.

In view of these characteristics, it was no surprise to those familiar with the model to see it competing very successfully in the production saloon car racing events which were so popular in the late 1950s.

Full production of the A35 continued until early 1959, at which time the saloon models were phased out in favour of the Farina styled A40 which had appeared late in 1958, and which itself utilised many of the mechanical elements of the A35. The fact that the new A40 was less suitable for adaptation to the small commercial vehicle role resulted in B.M.C. continuing to manufacture the A35 van into the late 1960s, and the closely related A35 Countryman also remained available until October 1962 when it finally gave way to a Countryman variation of the A40.

A35s were very popular, and successful, in production saloon car races during the late fifties. This is a support race to the 1959 British Grand Prix. (Courtesy L.A.T.)

Datapanel: Austin A30/A35

	A30	A35
Engine	4 cyl, ohv	4 cyl ohv
Capacity	803cc	948cc
Bore	58mm	62.9mm
Stroke	76.2mm	76.2mm
Compression ratio	7.2:1	8.3:1
Max BHP	28 @ 4800rpm	34 @ 4500rpm
Max torque	40lbs/ft @ 2400rpm	50lbs/ft @ 2000rpm
Gearing	13.3mph/1000rpm	14.2mph/1000rpm
Tyres	5.20 x 13	5.20 x 13
Kerb weight	14cwt	14cwt
Overall length	11ft 4 3/4in	11ft 4 3/4in
Overall width	4ft 7in	4ft 7in
Wheelbase	6ft 7 1/2in	6ft 7 1/2in

Performance

	"The Motor" road test, 2/6/54	"The Motor" 21/11/56
Max speed:		
Top gear	64.7mph (mean)	71.9mph (mean)
	67.2mph (best)	73.2mph (best)
3rd gear	42mph	58mph
2nd gear	27mph	33mph
Acceleration:		
0-30mph	8.5 seconds	6.8 seconds
0-40mph	14.5 seconds	11.6 seconds
0-50mph	24.5 seconds	18.7 seconds
0-60mph	42.3 seconds	30.1 seconds
	Top gear/3rd gear	Top gear/3rd gear
20-40mph	15.0/10.2 seconds	12.3/8.5 seconds
30-50mph	17.8/– seconds	14.1/11.5 seconds
40-60mph	28.2/– seconds	18.7/– seconds
Fuel consumption	43.5mpg (504 miles)	40.6mpg (380 miles)

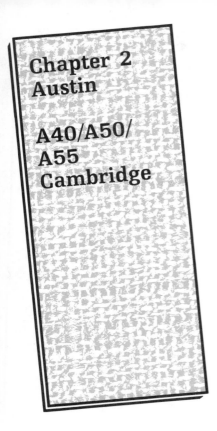

Chapter 2
Austin

A40/A50/ A55 Cambridge

Taking over from the successful Devon and Somerset series in September 1954, the new A40/A50 Cambridge was a notable step forward in many respects. A completely new monocoque body was employed, which, although slimmer than the preceding Somerset in external dimensions, did in fact offer greater internal width whilst at the same time taking advantage of a usefully longer wheelbase to seat the rear passengers ahead of the axle line. The adoption of integral construction also allowed a reduction in overall height, which was actually accompanied by a slight increase in headroom.

Unlike that of the company's smaller A30, the Cambridge bodyshell was not entirely of stressed skin construction, as it featured substantial longitudinal box section members welded to its floorpan on each side and running the full length of the car. The engine and rear spring mounting points were on these chassis type members, whilst the gearbox was attached to a short transverse bracing piece. A sturdy scuttle, and welded up front inner wings and front inner cross panel completed the front end structure. At the rear, the provision of inner wings and a high back panel aided overall rigidity. The wide boot lid had to be propped up by means of a stay, whereas the bonnet had the benefit of a self-supporting ratchet type arrangement. Housed in the boot, mounted transversely behind the rear seat and neatly boxed in, was an $8\frac{3}{4}$ gallon capacity fuel tank. The spare wheel was in a cradle beneath the luggage compartment, the cradle being wound down by the wheelbrace whenever the spare was required.

NEW THE AUSTIN CAMBRIDGE

Widest ever choice! 1200 c.c. or 1500 c.c. engines! Standard or de luxe interiors! 2- or 4-door! It's the greatest family motoring advance ever. You choose *exactly* the model to suit yourself.

Access to the passenger compartment was via four front-hinged doors on the A50, whilst in addition there was to be a two door alternative available on the A40 only. The doors were equipped with balanced drop type windows, but did have the advantage of swivelling quarter windows both front and rear. Both basic and De-Luxe models were available, the former being rather sparsely equipped, featuring just one sunvisor and a rubber floor-covering in the front, although carpeting was provided in the rear. The seating was upholstered in pvc, with the front seats being of the split bench type, each side of which was separately adjustable, although only to three fixed positions. Facing the driver was a sprung, T-spoked steering wheel. A binnacle on top of the steering column housed the speedometer and gauges for fuel level and engine temperature. Ahead of the front passenger was a useful lidded compartment, whilst a deep parcel shelf ran the full width of the car beneath the facia panel. De-Luxe equipment included twin sunvisors, door armrests, leather seat facings, a heater unit, and twin horns. Identifying the De-Luxe model externally were chrome window surrounds and bumper over-riders, these items being in addition to the plated door handles, bumpers, hubcaps and bootlid hinges of the basic model.

The designations A40 and A50 were applied depending upon which of the two engine options were installed in the Cambridge. The A40 unit was based on the well proven 1200cc engine of the previous A40 Somerset; and was in the same state of tune, producing 42bhp at 4500rpm, but now with some of the strengthened bottom end features which had been designed to cope with the increased capacity A50 unit. The 1200cc engine was also featuring new pistons equipped with four piston rings rather than the three of earlier models, this new arrangement being chosen in an attempt to lesson the sometimes rather high oil consumption of the original versions of this engine. The A50 engine was the larger bored, 1489cc version which in fact had already made its appearance in the BMC Morris Oxford Series II (see later chapter). Whereas in the respective Morris installations these B series units featured SU carburettors, Zenith instruments were to remain in the Austins. A Lockheed hydraulic clutch of $7\frac{1}{4}$ inch or 8 inch diameter, depending upon engine size, was operated by a pendant pedal. A new four-speed gearbox, with baulk ring type synchromesh between the three upper ratios, transmitted the power to a live rear axle via an open propeller shaft. Gear selection was by a column-mounted lever which, as it was now operating a rod type of linkage rather than the cable arrangement of the preceding model, gave rather more accurate control. New hypoid bevel final drives of

The "winged A" bonnet motif and the small separate sidelights of the new Austin Cambridge were small visible features carried over from the previous models.

Below. Recent photographs of a preserved A40 Cambridge De Luxe model. Note the unusual rear end styling.

5.125:1 and 4.875:1 gave overall gearing of 14.2mph:1000rpm and 15mph/1000rpm on the A40 and A50, respectively.

Cam and lever steering gear was once again employed; with the steering box, surprisingly, still being situated ahead of the axle line. Coil and wishbone independent front suspension now incorporated much larger shock-absorbers than previously. Both the front suspension units were conveniently mounted onto a detachable front crossmember whilst conventional leaf springs were mounted longitudinally to the chassis rails at the rear. Girling hydraulic brakes featured 9 inch diameter drums all round with shoes giving a total lining area of 121 square inches, these being activated by a similar pendant pedal to that of the clutch. The handbrake was controlled by a pistol grip lever which was neatly shrouded alongside the steering column. Completing the running gear were 15 inch diameter roadwheels with four-stud fixing shod with 5.60 section tyres. At prices of £649 (two door) and £664 for the A40, and £678 or £720 (De-Luxe) for the A50, the Cambridge represented sound value for money in this sector, with the two most obvious rivals being the Ford Consul (£666) and the slightly larger Vauxhall Wyvern at £702.

Weighing in at 20½cwt unladen, the Cambridge was similar in this respect to the Somerset, and as a result the A40 had a similar

A contemporary sales brochure illustration showing the two-door model.

performance, whereas the A50 did of course show a marked improvement. A maximum speed of around 75mph was accompanied by good top gear acceleration, with the 20 to 40mph and 30 to 50mph ranges being covered in an excellent 11 and 12 seconds, respectively, in this ratio. The fact that third gear was rather quicker than top up to around 50mph gave the A50 a marginally superior overtaking performance to its Ford and Vauxhall rivals in the important 30 to 50mph bracket. An overall fuel consumption of 28-30mpg was about average for this class of car. Rather curiously, in view of the larger shock-absorbers, the new Cambridge still displayed a degree of "float" over indifferent surfaces; a state of affairs which indicated that the damping was still not quite firm enough.

After only a matter of weeks in production, the semaphore indicators gave way to the more modern flashing type, the metal cover concealing the petrol cap received a lock, and all four passenger doors were equipped with window winding mechanisms. Several revisions to the A50 were announced in October 1956. An increase in the compression ratio to 8.3:1 raised the peak power output slightly, promising an improved performance/economy potential in conjunction with Premium grades of fuel. This change was accompanied by the introduction of lead-indium big-end bearings. The overall height of the car was reduced by 1 inch, this being achieved by adopting 13 inch diameter roadwheels fitted with larger section (5.90) tyres: a change which produced a subtle improvement in the car's overall appearance. The 5.90 x 13 tyres had a lower rolling radius than the superseded 5.60 x 15, and in order to compensate for this a new final drive ratio of 4.3:1 was adopted, this in fact serving to raise the overall gearing to 15.8mph/1000rpm.

Two new extra cost options were "Manumatic" two pedal

Below. Lowering the spare wheel tray by use of the starting handle.

Bottom. The interior arrangement of the Cambridge as first announced: the doors here being shown as equipped with simple balanced drop windows.

control of the solenoid operated clutch variety, and a Borg Warner
overdrive. With the latter item specified, the lower final drive ratio of
the A40 was used to bring the overdrive gearing on top gear to
manageable proportions for the four-cylinder engine.
19.9mph/1000rpm in overdrive top promised particularly relaxed
cruising and an excellent open road economy potential by 1½-litre
standards. In order to accommodate the overdrive, changes to the
floorpan had been necessary, and so, unfortunately, this denied the
owners of existing cars the opportunity of fitting this option
retrospectively. Prices had risen generally, and the A50 was now
priced at £772 or £820 in its De-Luxe guise, figures at which it was
still representing sound value. The smaller engined A40 was now
quietly deleted from the range.

In February 1957 the Cambridge was re-designated A55 upon
the introduction of several worthwhile improvements which affected
both the appearance and the convenience of the car. At the front, the
low set grille was now highlighted by a broad chromium surround,
and the headlamps acquired chrome rims of a hooded design. The
most distinguishing new feature however was the re-designed tail
end which added some 4 inches to the overall length whilst usefully
increasing the luggage compartment space. Loading was made easier

*The restyling which resulted in
the designation A55 is nicely
depicted in this reproduced
contemporary brochure.*

A CAR TO BE ADMIRED IN ANY COMPANY...

Clever design and careful attention to the smallest
detail have produced, in the A55 Saloon,
the proportion and sleek appearance attributed to
cars of much greater cost. From the
powerful double-dipping headlamps — hooded
with deep chromium rims — to the
combined reflectors, stop/tail lamps and
direction indicators blended neatly into
the rear end design, it is a masterpiece
of harmony which satisfies the eye and instills a
deep sense of pride of ownership.

Datapanel: Austin Cambridge A40/A50/A55

	A40 (A50)	A55
Engine	4 cyl, ohv	4 cyl, ohv
Capacity	1200cc (1489cc)	1489cc
Bore	65.4mm (73mm)	73mm
Stroke	89mm	89mm
Compression ratio	7.2:1	8.3:1
Max BHP	42 @ 4500rpm (50 @ 4400rpm)	51 @ 4250rpm
Max torque	78lbs/ft @ 2500rpm (58 @ 2400)	81lbs/ft @ 2000rpm
Gearing	14.2mph/1000rpm (15mph/1000rpm)	15.8mph/1000rpm
Tyres	5.60 x 15	5.90 x 13
Kerb weight	20 1/4cwt	20 3/4cwt
Overall length	13ft 6in	13ft 11in
Overall width	5ft 1 1/2in	5ft 1 1/2in
Wheelbase	8ft 3 1/4in	8ft 3 1/4in

Performance

	"The Autocar" road Test 8/4/55 (A50)	"The Motor" R/T No. 9/57 (Manumatic clutch)
Max speed:		
Top gear	71.7mph (mean) 75.0mph (best)	77.1/mph (mean) 81.8mph (best)
3rd gear	60mph	61mph
2nd gear	35mph	39mph
Acceleration:		
0-30mph	6.3 seconds	7.5 seconds
0-50mph	16.7 seconds	17.2 seconds
0-60mph	26.0 seconds	27.0 seconds
0-70mph	–	41.7 seconds
	Top gear/3rd gear	Top gear/3rd gear
20-40mph	10.7/7.4 seconds	12.6/8.2 seconds
30-50mph	12.0/10.3 seconds	14.6/9.6 seconds
40-60mph	15.7/– seconds	16.9/– seconds
50-70mph	–/– seconds	29.6/– seconds
Fuel consumption	28.4mpg (227 miles)	29.7mpg (443 miles)

The caption to this sales brochure picture read — "Distinctive facia styling is one of the delightful features of the A55 Saloon interior. Hand and foot controls are comfortably placed and, sitting in the driving seat the instruments are clearly visible through the two-spoke, 17-inch diameter steering wheel."

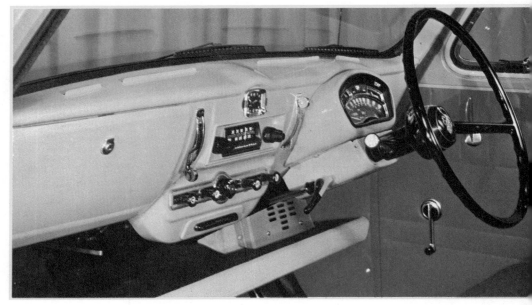

Smart two-tone paint combinations were available in the De Luxe A55 and were very much in vogue at the time.

now by the deletion of the high rear sill and the provision of a self supporting stay for the bootlid. A further useful touch was the provision of clips along the top of the petrol tank cover to which the jack and wheelbrace etc, could be attached, thus leaving an entirely unobstructed floor. A much wider rear screen was another welcome change, and the increased length of the car was further accentuated by a chromium flash running the full length of the bodywork, and in a position suitable for the new two tone paintwork variations which were now available for the modest extra cost of £15. Interior improvements were also evident. A padded facia top, a padded front edge to the parcel shelf, and a deeply-dished two-spoke steering wheel were all introduced with increased safety in mind. New front seats with an improved range of adjustment – ten positions over a 7 inch range – were a notable feature. Although now having more prominently shaped squabs, these seats were still full width and could be adjusted to allow three abreast seating whenever necessary. New chromium doorpulls were an addition to the normal armrests on the doors.

Naturally enough, these modifications had resulted in the Cambridge putting on a little more weight, and as the engine was also having to cope with the slightly higher gearing introduced earlier, the acceleration of this latest 1½-litre Austin did not show any real improvement over the original A50. It did however now have a usefully improved top speed – almost 80mph – and a corresponding increase in open road cruising ability, whilst still offering an overall 30mpg potential. As the prices were to remain the same £772 and £820 for the basic and De-Luxe models, the Cambridge was to continue to offer good value in this category, particularly so in its well-trimmed and equipped De-Luxe form. The range now continued in production until September 1958, at which time it was replaced by the completely re-bodied Farina styled A55 MkII.

Right. The engine compartment of the A55 – how simple and uncluttered they used to be!

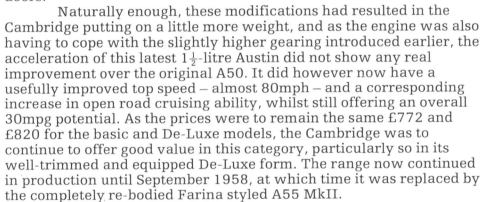

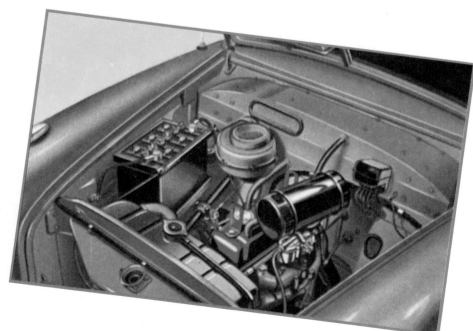

The completely new A90 Westminster, introduced in October 1954, followed the trend established some years earlier whereby the larger Austins would appear as scaled up versions of the company's medium sized models. Looking almost exactly like the Cambridge which had been released three weeks previously, the much larger Westminster bodyshell – also of similar monocoque construction – shared very little with the smaller model, only the four passenger doors in fact being interchangeable.

Both basic and De-Luxe models were to be available, with the former featuring pvc upholstery, carpeting in the rear compartment only, a single sunvisor and a single horn. The more comprehensive De-Luxe specification included leather seat facings, full carpeting, a pull down central armrest for the rear seat, pull down armrests on each side of each of the individual front seats which, as on the Cambridge, were of the full width type and so could be adjusted to form a bench type arrangement. Door mounted armrests, a passenger's sunvisor, twin horns and a heater unit were further De-Luxe items. The instrument housing contained two circular dials, one being the speedometer; which in this instance included a trip milometer in addition to the usual total mileage recorder. The other dial housing gauges for oil pressure, water temperature and fuel level. A usefully-sized glovebox – lockable on the De-Luxe – faced the front seat passenger, and a full width parcel shelf ran beneath the facia panel.

Luggage locker layout was also the same as on the recent smaller Austin, although now was of course appreciably more spacious with the extra width allowing a larger – 12½ gallon – transversely mounted fuel tank. A self supporting stay, as for the bonnet, now held the wide boot lid in the open position. External brightwork was similar to the Cambridge, but with the attractive addition of an almost full length side moulding, neatly styled at the rear to follow the wheel arch contour. Bumper over-riders were an additional De-Luxe feature only.

The most important advance over the superseded Hereford was to be found under the bonnet: now there was a six-cylinder engine unit. To be known as the "BMC C-Series", this engine also differed from the smaller A and B-series four-cylinder units in that it was in fact of Morris, rather than Austin design. Of conventional pushrod-operated ohv layout, the new engine featured a robust block with water jacketing around each individual cylinder, the bore of these being 79.4mm. Allied to this dimension was a piston stroke of 89mm which gave a total capacity of 2639cc. The forged steel crankshaft was fully counterbalanced and was supported by four main bearings. The fuel/air mixture was supplied by a single Zenith carburettor, and with a compression ratio of 7.3:1 the engine developed 85bhp at 4000rpm, with a very useful 130lbs/ft of torque being available at 2000rpm. These figures were more than ample to cope with this sturdy 25¾cwt car, and indicated that a lively performance was being offered. A 9 inch diameter hydraulic clutch was operated by a pendant pedal. The four-speed gearbox featured synchromesh between the three upper ratios, the selection of which was by a column-mounted lever. A rear axle ratio of 3.91:1, in conjunction with 15 inch diameter roadwheels and 6.40 section tyres resulted in sensibly high overall gearing of 19.8mph/1000rpm.

At the front, the suspension and steering set up was typically

Austin, with coil and wishbone independent suspension units and Bishop Cam steering gear arrangements. At the rear, the longitudinally mounted half-elliptic leaf springs were accompanied by a torsion anti-roll bar. The all hydraulic Girling braking system was notable for the fact that the large drums – 11 inch diameter – housed shoes which gave a total lining area of 180 square inches, an appreciably greater figure than was normal for this class of car at that time.

Perhaps the most surprising feature of the Westminster was that at its basic price of £791, or indeed at the £834 being asked for when in its well equipped De-Luxe configuration it was actually slightly cheaper than the preceding four-cylinder Hereford model. At these prices the Westminster was in direct competition with the well established Ford Zephyr/Zodiac and Vauxhall Velox/Cresta ranges. On the road, the big Austin was quicker than either of these two rivals, with a maximum speed in excess of 85mph and a 0 to 60mph capability of around 18 seconds. Being rather higher geared than these however, it could not quite match their excellent top gear flexibility, but it did have the advantage of a third gear ratio which gave a comfortable 60mph or so, and was thus a most useful overtaking gear. Its braking performance too was excellent, and all of this was accompanied by good riding characteristics and more than just adequate handling qualities.

An overall fuel consumption of 21/22mpg was perfectly reasonable for what was quite a heavy car, and these figures could be improved upon later, when towards the end of 1955, a Borg Warner overdrive became an optional extra. A lower axle ratio, 4.1:1, was used if the overdrive was specified, giving 18.9mph/1000rpm in direct top whilst still providing a long legged 27mph/1000rpm in overdrive. Curiously, the manual control with which to lock-out the semi-automatic Borg Warner device was situated under the passenger side of the facia.

At Silverstone, in May 1956, Ken Wharton had thrilled the crowd with his display in the Production Touring Car Race in which his BMC works-prepared Westminster had engaged in a race long battle with Ivor Bueb's Mk VII Jaguar. This particular Westminster, with a cylinder head re-worked by tuning expert Harry Weslake and sporting three twin-choke Weber carburettors, was indeed a very potent machine.

An excellent surviving example of the early Westminster model, with only the reflective number plate giving any indication that this is a recent photograph.

Showpiece

NEW THE AUSTIN WESTMINSTER

The pace-maker! New, surging power—from a brand-new six-cylinder engine! New longer, lower, sleeker lines! New roomier, spread-yourself comfort. Extra large luggage compartment. This Westminster is news!

AUSTIN
—you can depend on it!

THE AUSTIN MOTOR COMPANY LIMITED • LONGBRIDGE • BIRMINGHAM

A 1954 Motor Show advertisement depicting the new A90 Westminster. Once again a considerable amount of artistic licence is in evidence.

Later the same month, a high-performance top-of-the-range model was announced, which, whilst not in the racing tune of Wharton's car, was said to have been developed on similar lines which took into account the experiences of the competition department. Designated the A105, this latest version was recognizable in its two tone paint finish, applied in a "sandwich" scheme. Stainless steel wheel discs, chromed hooded headlamp rims, twin spotlights, twin wing mirrors, and whitewall tyres were further distinguishing features. Improved interior trim included new front seats, each of which was an inch wider than before, and which were styled to look exactly like a bench seat when set in the same position. A padded facia top, covered in leathercloth, and a half horn ring

The luxurious A105 appeared early in 1956. The production version differed very slightly from the prototype car depicted here in that the two-tone paintwork division continued down to wheel-arch level at the rear.

Two surviving examples of the later A105 are pictured here. VYO 917 in fact being one of the rare Vanden-Plas models.

replacing the central button were other new features.

Engine modifications for the A105 included an improved cylinder head and high compression pistons which raised the compression ratio to 8.25:1. Double valve springs, and twin SU carburettors connected to a large oil-bath air cleaner were further departures from standard, as was also a re-worked exhaust system which reduced back pressure. These changes resulted in 102bhp at 4600rpm being accompanied by 142lbs/ft torque at 2000rpm; a substantial increase over the basic model's figures of 85bhp and 130lbs/ft torque. The four speed gearbox retained the column mounted change, and the transmission was complete with the Borg Warner overdrive and its associated 4.11:1 rear axle. Suspension modifications were confined to shortened front coil springs and revised camber rear leaf springs, this treatment serving to lower the

A period advertisement shows off well the increased length of the A95 and also features the Countryman.

Power takes beautiful new shape

THE NEW A.95 WITH NEW EXTRA POWER

By Appointment to Her Majesty
Queen Elizabeth II
Motor Car Manufacturers
The Austin Motor Company Limited

NEW A.95 SALOON. Sparkling performance, good looks, and superb comfort are what you notice first about this exciting new car from Austin. It's a car for the motorist who likes to travel far and fast, and to arrive fresh and relaxed. The A.95 has ample room for five, ample leg-room for six-footers because of the new long wheelbase. Its boot is vast and very easy to load. Its 6-cylinder 2.6 litre ohv engine is extremely economical. And for all its power it's beautifully quiet and smooth. New features include a padded dashboard, improved steering wheel, wrap-round rear window to cut out blind spots. Basic price £695 plus £348 17s. purchase tax. And it can

have an automatic gearbox or overdrive as extras. NEW A.95 COUNTRYMAN. Below, Austin's big new estate car, shooting brake, or station wagon. But whatever you call it the A.95 Countryman is more than just a fetcher and carrier. It's enormously useful and enormously roomy. It's handsome, comfortable, swift. It's a car to tour in; you can sleep in it in luxury. It has the same superb engine, the same finish throughout, as you get in the A.95 saloon. It is indeed an Austin to be proud of.

Price **£810** plus £406 7s. purchase tax.

One last word : these cars carry a twelve-month warranty.

Buy **AUSTIN** and be proud of it

THE AUSTIN MOTOR COMPANY LIMITED, LONGBRIDGE, BIRMINGHAM.

A105 by more than one inch, thus giving a subtle improvement in the car's overall appearance as a bonus on top of the beneficial effect on the handling qualities.

With a maximum speed of 95mph coupled with the ability to accelerate from rest to 80mph in only 30 seconds, the A105 was definitely in the high-performance category in 1956. Although the price had broken the £1000 barrier, the A105 being listed at £1,109, with this performance being accompanied by a very comprehensive level of equipment and a high trim and finish standard, the A105 Westminster could still be considered excellent value.

Further changes to the entire range were announced in October 1956. The basic model now received the high compression ratio of the A105, but retained the single Zenith carburettor. With 92bhp now being developed, the designation A95 was adopted for the basic model. The A105 power unit remained unchanged, and both models could now be supplied with a Borg Warner automatic gearbox, with which option the standard 3.9:1 axle ratio was retained. Identifying these updated models were several notable bodywork and exterior brightwork changes. A re-styled grille; its extremities now extending to embrace the flashing indicators, and chromed hooded headlamp rims – as previously on the A105 only – were new front end features. Considerably longer rear wing pressings increased the overall length of the car by 10 inches, whilst at the same time allowing the rear wheels to be set a little further back, thus increasing the wheelbase by 2 inches. This in turn allowed the rear seats to be re-positioned slightly more rearwards with a consequent improvement in rear compartment leg room. An unusually roomy luggage boot was now provided, and loading was made easier than hitherto by the deletion of the high back panel. Accentuating the lengthy appearance was a new chrome side-moulding treatment in which two almost full length strips were placed just sufficiently far apart to accommodate a contrasting colour, this "flash" of colour

On display at Earls Court in 1956, the new A95 Countryman, complete with roof rack in this picture.

AUSTIN A95 COUNTRYMAN

*Additional embellishments
continued to be a feature of the
top-of-the-range Westminster
and are featured strongly in
this contemporary
advertisement.*

when applied, giving a "speedy" look to the car. A wider rear
window, and completely re-styled bumpers completed the updated
specification.

Announced simultaneously was an estate car version, with
the mechanical specification and trim level of the A95 and named
Countryman, as was usually the case with the Austin estates.
Retaining the four passenger door layout, with the rear doors just
being squared up slightly, and a nicely raked horizontally split
tailgate, the big Countryman looked quite sleek by estate car
standards. In addition to the usual estate car convenience was an
arrangement whereby folding the rear seat in a particular way
resulted in a double berth sleeping area with the rear seat squab
forming a pillow. The 4.11:1 axle was the only ratio available on the
Countryman and was used in conjunction with larger, 6.70 x 15
tyres.

With prices now of £1043 (A95), £1199 (A105) and £1216
(Countryman), the six-cylinder Austins had moved somewhat up-
market, and whilst perhaps not now representing outstanding value
for money, were nevertheless excellent cars.

Mention of a racing Westminster has already been made, and
in 1958 the full performance potential of the model was amply
demonstrated by top saloon car driver Jack Sears. Driving a BMC
works-prepared car, which was actually based on the earlier short
wheelbase model, Sears gained outright victory in the first BRSCC
saloon car championship in an exciting season's racing in which the
big Austin had triumphed after some memorable "dices" with Jeff
Uren's Ford Zephyr.

A limited production edition of the Westminster also appeared
in 1958 – the Austin A105 Vanden Plas. Partly finished saloons,
painted in either black, maroon, or grey, and each with a metallic
grey "flash", were delivered without interior trim to the Kingsbury

works of coachbuilding specialists Vanden Plas. Here, the Westminsters were trimmed in a most luxurious manner. Figured walnut was applied to the door cappings and to a re-styled facia. A woollen headlining, with a sponge rubber backing, was fitted, and deep-pile carpeting covered the floor. Deeply upholstered hide seating finished off the luxury treatment, the whole of which was either in tan or blue. £1474 was being asked for this exclusive Austin, a price which did of course take it out of the family car bracket and put it alongside some well established luxury models.

The Westminster range now continued in production until September 1959 when the A95/A105 gave way to the much larger Farina styled, 2.9-litre A99 Westminster.

Datapanel: Austin Westminster A90/A95/A105

	A90	A95 (A105)
Engine	6 cyl, ohv	6 cyl, ohv
Capacity	2639cc	2639cc
Bore	79.4mm	79.4mm
Stroke	89mm	89mm
Compression ratio	7.3:1	8.25:1
Max BHP	85 @ 4000rpm	92 @ 4500rpm (102 @ 4600rpm)
Max torque	130lbs/ft @ 2000rpm	130lbs/ft @ 2000rpm (142 @ 2600)
Gearing	19.8mph/1000rpm	19.8mph/1000rpm (18.9/1000 in top) (27/1000 in O/Drive)
Tyres	6.40 x 15	6.40 x 15
Kerb weight	25 1/2cwt	26 3/4cwt
Overall length	14ft 3in	15ft 1in
Overall width	5ft 4in	5ft 4in
Wheelbase	8ft 7 3/4in	8ft 10in (A105 between May '56 & Oct' '56 had same length, width & wheelbase as on A90 model)

Performance

	"The Motor" road test No/ 9/55	"The Motor" road test No. 8/58 (A95 Countryman)
Max speed:		
Top gear	85.7mph (mean) 86.1mph (best)	91.2mph (mean) 93.7mph (best)
3rd gear	70mph	75mph
2nd gear	49mph	46mph
Acceleration:		
0-30mph	5.2 seconds	5.2 seconds
0-50mph	12.5 seconds	12.5 seconds
0-60mph	18.9 seconds	17.6 seconds
0-70mph	28.5 seconds	26.0 seconds
0-80mph	47.2 seconds	42.1 seconds
	Top gear/3rd gear	Top gear/3rd gear
20-40mph	9.3/6.6 seconds	9.9/6.9 seconds
30-50mph	10.7/7.7 seconds	11.1/8.1 seconds
40-60mph	12.5/9.9 seconds	13.1/9.6 seconds
50-70mph	16.0/19.0 seconds	16.1/14.1 seconds
60-80mph	26.2/– seconds	25.2/– seconds
Fuel consumption	20.2mpg (1330 miles)	20.5mpg (930 miles)

Chapter 3
Ford

Anglia/ Prefect/ Popular (E494A, E493A and 103E)

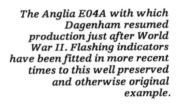

The Anglia E04A with which Dagenham resumed production just after World War II. Flashing indicators have been fitted in more recent times to this well preserved and otherwise original example.

Of all the manufacturers offering inexpensive family saloons, only the Ford Motor Company entered the 1950s still producing what was basically a pre-war range of cars. At the bottom end of the range was the Anglia E494A. Apart from the bodywork, which was based very closely on that of the 8hp model 7Y of 1937, much of the remainder of the Anglia could be traced right back to the original 8hp Y type of 1932.

A simple chassis frame of open longitudinal members and similar transverse stiffeners, housed typical Ford running gear with the suspension arrangements for each axle being a single transverse leaf spring. The Girling braking system was rod operated, and featured 10 inch diameter drums all round containing shoes with an ample total lining area of 85 square inches. Worm and nut steering gear, and 17 inch diameter roadwheels with 4.50 section tyres completed this aspect of the mechanical specification.

The sidevalve engine had bore and stroke measurements of 56.6mm and 92.5mm respectively, giving a capacity of 933cc. With its single carburettor and a compression ratio of 6.3:1, the unit developed 23bhp at 4000rpm. The transmission consisted of a mechanically operated clutch and a three-speed gearbox with synchromesh between the upper two ratios. Gear selection was by a long floor-mounted lever, and the drive to the spiral bevel rear axle assembly was by Ford's usual torque tube arrangement. A final drive ratio of 5.5:1 gave overall gearing of 13.8mph/1000rpm. A 6 volt electrical system, and vacuum operated windscreen wipers were also in accordance with established Ford practice.

Offering very ample room for four people was the quite smoothly styled two door bodywork. Folding squabs on the separate front seats allowed easy access to the rear via the very wide front hinged doors. Both doors were fitted with winding windows, and in fact the Anglia was surprisingly well equipped by economy car standards at that time. Twin wipers with a vacuum reservoir, twin sunvisors, self cancelling trafficators, a sprung steering wheel and a fully carpeted floor were all standard features. The seating, door covering and side panels were in leathercloth. A moulded plastic dashboard contained a large centrally mounted speedometer around which was grouped the switchgear. A full width parcel shelf ran beneath the facia panel.

The bonnet top was split along the centre-line, enabling each side – including the bonnet side – to be opened independently: although the low mounting of the engine and the rather high wings did not make for particularly easy access. At the rear, the small luggage boot featured a drop-down lid which was held by adjustable straps, a useful arrangement which allowed bulky objects to be carried with the boot lid open, but adjusted to whatever angle was necessary to contain the load. The spare wheel was housed beneath a false boot floor, and beneath the spare was a 7 gallon fuel tank, the neck of which protruded through the nearside rear bodywork. Silver painted wheels with chrome hubcaps, chrome bumpers complete with over-riders, chrome door handles and a thin chromium surround for the grille and bonnet side louvres finished off the Anglia's neat external appearance.

The performance included a maximum speed of virtually 60mph and an ability to reach 50mph from rest in 38 seconds: figures which, in 1950, would enable it to maintain station with the traffic stream comfortably. Cruising at around 45mph would return better than 40mpg. Handling qualities were not up to the standards being set by the new postwar rivals, but at its tax-paid price of £310 the Anglia represented an excellent, well proven new car bargain, and would in fact continue to make many more new friends before its eventual demise.

In production alongside the Anglia was the 10hp model E493A; the Prefect. Built on a similar chassis and running gear, but with a 4 inch longer wheelbase (7ft 10in), the Prefect offered four door convenience and rather more rear compartment knee room than its shorter stablemate. Under the bonnet was the famous 1172cc version of Dagenham's small sidevalve unit, the increase in capacity being achieved by enlarging the bore diameter to 63.5mm. Still retaining a single Zenith carburettor, and with a modest compression ratio of 6.16:1 the 1172cc engine produced 30bhp at 4000rpm, a very useful increase over the Anglia, and more than just sufficient to compensate for the weight penalty of almost 2cwt that was imposed by the larger four door bodywork. The transmission was as on the Anglia, including the rear axle ratio, although, in fact the larger engined car was pulling slightly lower overall gearing. This was due to the adoption of larger, 5.00 section tyres which were now however fitted on smaller diameter (16 inch) rims.

On the road, the Prefect showed a marked improvement over

ANGLIA

PREFECT

EARLS COURT · OCT 17-27 · STAND No153

48

the Anglia in terms of acceleration, bringing down the 0-50mph time by some 12 or 13 seconds, and thus enabling the similar 60mph or so maximum speed to be appreciably more usable than on the smaller car. Fuel consumption suffered slightly, although if cruising was restricted to around 40mph an overall journey figure of 40mpg was possible, and at its price of £371 the Prefect was also something of a bargain. A re-designed front-end, featuring built-in headlamps, had considerably updated the Prefect's appearance late in 1949, and Dagenham's pre-war small-car range was set to continue well into the 1950s.

Dagenham's other product in 1950, the large, V8-engined Pilot was also almost wholly a 1930s car. Big, powerful, and quite lavishly equipped, the Pilot, with its £764 price tag and 14/15mpg economy was not really competing in the inexpensive family car market, and was destined to be replaced by the less expensive Zephyr Six in 1951.

When the Anglia and Prefect finally gave way to the new 100E models in 1953, it was not however the end of the line for the "upright" Fords. Although announced on the eve of the 1953 Earls Court Show as a "new" model, the Ford Popular 103E was a very familiar looking car. Higher rates of purchase tax, coupled with increases in the cost of raw materials had resulted generally in more expensive cars. The new Anglia 100E was over £500, but Ford were still keen to be offering the least expensive "real" car on the market.

Priced at £391, the new Popular was in effect a de-trimmed Anglia E494A but fitted with the 1172cc engine previously only available on the export Anglia and the Prefect. The de-trimming exercise was quite extensive. Painted bumpers (now without over-riders), painted hubcaps, smaller headlamps and a carriage key to open the boot were all economy features. Inside the boot, the false floor over the spare wheel was omitted, actually slightly improving the luggage capacity. Only the driver's seat was now adjustable, whilst only that for the front passenger could be tipped forward for access to the rear. Both doors retained their wind down windows, but the door trims were now plainly styled, the seat trim was cheaper and a plastic coated felt replaced the previous carpeting. No sunvisors were fitted, and only the driver had the benefit of a windscreen wiper which itself was now without the vacuum reservoir. Three circular instruments, a large speedometer flanked by an ammeter and fuel gauge, were set into the painted steel dash panel. The instruments were viewed through a three spoked sprung steering wheel which now looked rather out of place in the austere surroundings.

Although obviously very basic, the Popular was an attractive proposition for many who would otherwise be forced to buy on the second-hand market, and its low purchase price was perhaps more than anything else responsible for its lengthy production run. Late in 1955 production was transferred to the former Briggs Motor Bodies plant at Doncaster, Ford having acquired the Briggs concern sometime earlier. Apart from very minor changes, such as twin rear lamps and a cheaper steering wheel, the Popular continued unchanged until finally deleted in August 1959, at which time the price was still a mere £419.

The Ford Popular 103E (often quite wrongly referred to as E93A), the last of a long line of remarkably inexpensive, but "real" motor cars.

The simple facia layout of the Popular. Some of the early 103E models featured the sprung steering wheel of the previous Anglia/Prefect cars – presumably simply using up remaining stocks.

Datapanel: Ford Anglia/Prefect/Popular E494A/E493A/103E

	Anglia (Prefect)	Popular
Engine	*4 cyl, Sidevalve*	*4 cyl, Sidevalve*
Capacity	*933cc (1172cc)*	*1172cc*
Bore	*56.6mm (63.5mm)*	*63.5mm*
Stroke	*92.5mm*	*92.5mm*
Compression ratio	*6.3:1 (6.16:1)*	*6.16:1*
Max BHP	*23.4 @ 4000rpm (30.1 @ 4000 rpm)*	*30.1 @ 4000rpm*
Gearing	*13.8mph/1000rpm (13.5mph/1000rpm)*	*13.8mph/1000rpm*
Tyres	*4.50 x 17 (5.00 x 16)*	*4.50 x 17*
Kerb weight	*14 3/4cwt (16 3/4cwt)*	*14 1/2cwt*
Overall length	*12ft 10in (13ft)*	*12ft 8in*
Overall width	*4ft 9in*	*4ft 9in*
Wheelbase	*7ft 6in (7ft 10in)*	*7ft 6in*

Performance

	"The Motor" R/T No. 20/49 Anglia	"The Motor" R/T No.15/54
Max speed:		
Top gear	*57.2mph (mean)* *62.9mph (best)*	*60.3mph (mean)* *60.8mph (best)*
2nd gear	*40mph*	*41mph*
1st gear	*–*	*24mph*
Acceleration:		
0-30mph	*9.6 seconds*	*8.6 seconds*
0-50mph	*38.3 seconds*	*24.1 seconds*
	Top gear/2nd gear	Top gear/2nd gear
20-40mph	*16.7/13.6 seconds*	*11.9/10.5 seconds*
30-50mph	*28.8/– seconds*	*15.3/– seconds*
Fuel consumption	*36.2mpg (470 miles)*	*36.4mpg (506 miles)*

Chapter 3
Ford

Consul/
Zephyr Six/
Zephyr-
Zodiac Mk1

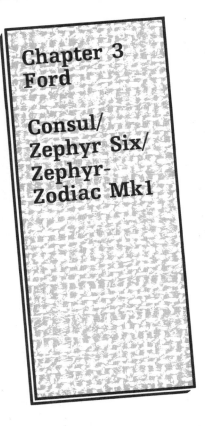

1950 Motor Show advert for the new Consul and Zephyr Six. The styling was based loosely on the big 1949 American Ford, scaled down for the Dagenham cars. In contemporary advertising Ford pushed the value-for-money offered by their cars.

As the result of an intensive two year development programme which had begun in 1948, the Ford Motor Co. of Dagenham unveiled their completely new Consul (4-cylinder) and Zephyr Six at the Earls Court Motor Show in October 1950.

In almost every respect traditional Ford thinking had been abandoned, and Dagenham had produced a quite revolutionary new range, the features of which, such as the three box body style, short stroked engines, MacPherson strut independent front suspension, and pendant foot pedals, would however, eventually be so widely copied as to render this unique specification absolutely conventional some twenty years later.

Of monocoque construction, the bodyshell was the first to be designed around the strut type independent front suspension which was the brainchild of American Ford engineer, Earle MacPherson. Sturdy front inner wings were welded along their rear edge to a substantial scuttle/bulkhead structure, and were also linked to the scuttle by welded-in tie bars running diagonally across the engine bay. The suspension strut upper mountings were incorporated into the inner wings at the point where the tie bars were welded in. The struts being located at the bottom by a transverse anti-roll bar and track control arms attached to a crossmember fixed to the chassis rails which were welded into the lower edge of the inner wings. This arrangement transferred the suspension loads into the scuttle/bulkhead structure and from there into the floorpan, and, via the windscreen pillars, into the roof. The structural arrangements at the front were completed with another welded in bulkhead with a large aperture to take the radiator. A bolted on front panel housed the radiator grille and was unstressed, as were the bolt-on front wings.

Below. An early production Consul shown in a contemporary press release photograph.

The whole front end structure differed slightly in length according to whether the 4 or 6-cylinder engine was to be installed. Access to the engine bay was by a wide rear-hinged bonnet which was held in the open position by a ratchet type stay.

From the windscreen rearwards both the Consul and Zephyr bodyshells were identical, with the full width passenger compartment providing excellent accommodation for four people and adequate room for six. At the rear, access to a large and conveniently-shaped luggage boot was by a full width counterbalanced lid, although luggage did have to be be lifted over a rather high back panel, the height of which was chosen for its important contribution to the rear end rigidity of the car. The spare wheel was mounted in an upright position in the right-hand side of the boot, from where it could be removed with the minimum of disturbance of any luggage being carried. A nine gallon fuel tank was situated centrally under the boot floor, protected on each side by the rear chassis members welded into the floor, and was thus virtually immune from the effects of a rear

1954 Zephyr Six in a wintry setting. The re-styled bumpers and chrome side strips introduced the previous year are evident here.

The facia panel phased in during 1952. The horn-ring was only a feature of the six-cylinder models.

Zephyr Six
Convertible-de-Ville

Ford '5-Star' Motoring ★ the best at lowest cost

end side swipe. Protection of the bodywork at both front and rear was by strong bumper bars, their mounting brackets being bolted directly on to the ends of the chassis members.

The bumpers, hubcaps, grille, script, lamp surrounds, and door handles were chrome plated on both models, and additional chrome embellishment on the Zephyr Six included window surrounds, rear numberplate lamp cover, front wing flashes, a bonnet motif, and bumper over-riders. The styling of these new Fords appeared to be a very subtle scale down of the first all new post war American Ford which had appeared during 1948, and indeed, the parent Company in Detroit had insisted that Dagenham's new cars should reflect this new American Ford image.

A large glass area gave good all round vision and a reasonably light and airy effect to the interior, although the latter effect was offset somewhat by the choice of a rather dark coloured cloth roof lining. The twin sunvisors were also covered in the same material.

A simple facia panel housed a stylish speedometer and mileage recorder immediately in front of the driver: this instrument also containing the fuel gauge and an ammeter. A small lidded glovebox in front of the passenger matched the shape of the instrument housing.

A Zodiac advertisement which suggests that 1954 would be a a year to remember. It was – just ask any Mk. I enthusiast today ...

Vintage 1954

In every community there are people who have a flair for good-living, a sense of style. That it is such people who have made the Zephyr Zodiac the most admired car of recent years tells you a great deal about the car itself. If you have just discovered the exhilaration of '5-Star' motoring, you will find 1954 a year to remember.

THE *Zephyr* ZODIAC IS A LOVELY CAR

Ford '5 Star' Motoring ★ *the best at lowest cost*

A recent photograph of a surviving example of one of the rare Farnham estate cars. This particular Consul took its owner and family on a trip to France in 1984, showing how practical these cars are even in the 1980s.

Both cars featured a sprung T-spoked steering wheel, that of the Zephyr Six adorned with an elegant chrome plated ring with which to sound its twin horn installation; the Consul's single horn being sounded by a button in the steering wheel boss. The bench seats were upholstered in pvc, as were the door trims. Swivelling front quarter windows, and window winding mechanism in all four doors were provided. Additionally, on the Zephyr doors only, were padded armrests/doorpulls. The Zephyr also featured fully fitted carpeting, whereas the Consul's floorcovering was in moulded rubber.

Twin windscreen wipers (still vacuum operated in the Ford tradition, but now with the benefit of a booster pump) and self cancelling semaphore trafficators were standard equipment in both cases, and available as extra cost options were a heater and demisting unit, radio, and leather upholstery.

Power for the Consul and Zephyr Six was provided by completely new pushrod-operated overhead valve engines in 4 and 6-cylinder configuration. These units were the first type to go into production in which the measurement of the cylinder bore was greater than that of the piston stroke. This short stroke, or oversquare arrangement as it was also called, had many natural advantages but had hitherto been avoided due to nonsensical road tax regulations in which engines were taxed according to the size of the bore. However, a new flat rate of annual duty for all cars was now in force, and the engineers at Dagenham had taken full advantage of this situation. The bore and stroke measurements chosen, 79.3mm x 76.2mm, resulted in total cylinder capacities of 1508cc and 2262cc for the 4 and 6-cylinder units, and allowed the engines to run at only 500ft/min piston speed per 1000rpm. The short piston stroke in turn required only a short crankshaft throw, and consequently a generous main and big end bearing journal overlap was possible; thus ensuring an extremely rigid shaft. Both crankshafts were fully counterbalanced, and ran in three (4-cylinder) or four (6-cylinder) main bearings.

Mixture was provided by a single Zenith carburettor in both cases, and with a compression ratio of 6.8:1 the Consul engine produced 47bhp at 4400rpm and 72lbs.ft torque at 2300rpm, the corresponding figures for the Zephyr Six being 68bhp at 4000rpm and 108lbs/ft at 2000rpm, ample figures with which to cope with kerb weights of $21\frac{3}{4}$ and $23\frac{1}{2}$ cwt.

The 8 inch diameter clutch was hydraulically operated for the first time on a Dagenham car, but the three speed gearbox with synchronisation between the upper two ratios only was very much in the Ford tradition. Selection of the ratios was by a steering column-mounted lever which was to become widely regarded as the best of its type. An open propeller shaft replaced Ford's previous torque tube drive, and transmitted the power to new hypoid rear axle assemblies with ratios of 4.625:1 and 4.375:1 respectively for the 4 and 6-cylinder cars. These ratios gave relatively low overall gearing of 14.9mph/1000rpm on the Consul and 16.3mph/1000rpm on the Zephyr Six, and were chosen in order to provide exceptional top gear acceleration and hill-climbing abilities.

Complementing the MacPherson strut set up at the front, was Burman worm and peg steering gear. The steering box itself was placed well behind the front axle line in such a position as to make it virtually impossible for the steering column to be pushed towards the driver's chest in a frontal collision: a valuable safety feature which would, eventually, be widely copied. The rear suspension consisted of longitudinally mounted leaf springs and lever arm shock absorbers. An all hydraulic Girling braking system was employed, and featured 9 inch diameter drums on all four wheels with shoes of 1.75 inch width giving a total lining area of 121 square inches, 13 inch diameter roadwheels with 5.90 and 6.40 section tyres on the Consul and Zephyr respectively completed the then very advanced specification.

Priced at £543 and £608 on their introduction, very few of these cars reached the home market before the April 1951 budget in which purchase tax was doubled. However, at the new tax paid prices of £717 and £816 the Consul and Zephyr Six offered unrivalled value in 1951.

Just as the specification suggested, the new Fords proved to have a performance and general roadworthiness which set new levels for this type and price of car. The Consul could exceed 70mph by a useful margin and would accelerate from rest to 60mph in 26 seconds. Top gear flexibility was excellent by 4-cylinder standards, with a 20 to 40mph time in this ratio of 12 seconds. Cruising at 50mph would return 30mpg and even consistently hard driving was

A 1955 Consul awaits delivery.

Its whitewall tyres, sunvisor and pillar-mounted spotlamp typifying the fifties scene, this 1954 overdrive-equipped Zephyr Six pauses at a modern motorway service area – 30 years after leaving Dagenham.

Zephyr Zodiac. Glamorous, luxurious, powerful and yours for just £851 in 1954. Whitewall tyres reflect the strong American influence in car styling making itself felt at the time.

unlikely to produce a figure worse than 25mpg. The Zephyr Six could go from rest to 60 and 70mph in 20 and 30 seconds respectively, and continue very quickly to a maximum of 80mph. The flexibility of the six-cylinder engine allowed rapid acceleration from below 15mph in top gear, and the Zephyr required less than 9 seconds to go from 20 to 40mph in this ratio. In the same gear it could also climb hills of the 1 in 7 variety and reach 70mph on an uphill gradient of 1 in 20. 22/23mpg overall accompanied this impressive performance, and for those who normally kept much of the Zephyr's ample power in reserve 27/28mpg was within reach.

In answer to criticism levelled at the lack of stowage space in the front, a completely new facia, incorporating a deep full width parcel shelf, was a feature of the Consul and Zephyr models on the Ford stand at Earls Court in 1951, but was not in fact phased into production until the summer of 1952. In November 1952 a change in the Consul's axle ratio to 4.556:1 raised the overall gearing slightly to 15.3mph/1000rpm, giving a small but useful increase in fuel economy with 32/33mpg now being possible at 50mph. A revised ratio of 4.444:1 gave the Zephyr Six very slightly lower gearing, now 16.1mph/1000rpm, thus sharpening its acceleration but without any loss in maximum speed as the engine would rev a little harder in the lower gear.

In the hands of Ken Wharton, a Consul had won the Dutch International Tulip Rally in 1952, and in January 1953 this deservedly popular range reached new heights of prestige when a standard model Zephyr Six, driven by Dutchman Maurice Gatsonides, won the Monte Carlo Rally.

Convertible models became available during 1953, having been developed by specialists Carbodies of Coventry. A substantial X-bracing frame was welded into the standard floorpan, this being necessary in order to compensate for the inevitable loss of rigidity which resulted from the removal of the stressed steel roof. On the Zephyr Six, the hood was power operated to and from the half way — De-Ville — position. Priced at £808, the Consul convertible was undercut by the slightly smaller Austin Somerset and Hillman Minx drophead models which were attractively priced at £705 and £723. At £960 however, the Zephyr Six convertible was unopposed. Both purchase tax and factory economies had by now reduced the price of the saloons to £666 and £754.

These prices remained unchanged when at Earls Court in 1953 a facelift comprising deeper, restyled bumpers, new bonnet mascots, full length chrome strips along the waistline, and re-styled door trims and seating was announced. Far more significant however, was a remarkably comprehensively equipped addition to the range which was also on show — the Zephyr Zodiac — priced at just £851. Two tone paintwork, 9 carat gold plated script, twin wing mirrors, fog and spot lamps, reversing lamp, lockable fuel filler cap, chrome wheelrim embellishers and whitewall tyres immediately identified this impressive newcomer. Interior appointments included two tone leather upholstery, a woollen headlining, cigar lighter, vanity mirror, and electric clock. The heater unit was standard equipment, as were windscreen washers, heavy duty battery, and a high compression ratio (7.5:1) cylinder head which raised the power output to 71bhp. This cylinder head, which required the use of Premium grades of fuel, was also to be available on the Zephyr Six as a no cost option, whilst the hard wearing qualities of both the 4 and 6-cylinder units were further improved by the adoption of chrome plated top piston rings. Self cancelling flashing trafficators had recently made their Ford debut on the new Anglia and Prefect 100E models, and this arrangement now completed the up-date on the Consul/Zephyr/Zodiac range.

In September 1954 a clutch pedal assist spring was introduced on the 6-cylinder models, resulting in lighter clutch operation, and interior trim changes included a washable vinyl headlining for the Zodiac and an improved cloth lining with a tighter weave for the Zephyr. New rear lamp surrounds, incorporating a square-shaped reflector above the light unit were now a feature of all three cars. An estate car conversion of the Zephyr Six by the coachbuilders E.D. Abbott of Farnham in Surrey was displayed at Earls Court in October 1954. Priced at £145, the conversion could be carried out on any existing Consul/Zephyr/Zodiac and had the full approval of the Ford Motor Co.

A wide variety of performance conversions for both the 4 and 6-cylinder models were available by this time from specialist tuning firms. Modified cylinder heads, twin and triple carburettor inlet manifolds, and 4 and 6 branch exhaust systems allowed varying degrees of increased speed and acceleration. Former racing driver, BRM boss Raymond Mays, himself an enthusiastic Zephyr owner since 1951, had first offered a re-worked cylinder head/triple SU Zephyr conversion in 1953 for £75. The three siamesed inlet ports in the standard cylinder head were, however, a limiting factor as far as extreme power outputs were concerned and Mays now introduced a conversion which consisted of a light alloy cylinder head with six separate inlet ports, a twin SU arrangement, and a complete dual exhaust system. Priced at £100, this conversion produced 106bhp at 5000rpm which was sufficient to just put the Zephyr into the genuine 100mph category.

Following the Monte Carlo win in 1953, "works" Zephyrs had contested several international rallies in which they took a further 9 class awards. In May 1955 a private entrant, Vic Preston, drove a standard Zephyr to outright victory in the East African Safari Rally.

Technical changes phased in during 1955 were a modified pick-up pipe for the oil pump, as a result of which the pump now became self-priming, and an oil-filled ignition coil. In August that year the Borg Warner semi automatic overdrive became available as a factory fitted optional extra on the 6-cylinder models only. This option now meant a choice of no less than three such fittings, as the Laycock de-Normanville overdrive and Handa overdrive had been available through specialist outlets with fitting kits for the Consul/Zephyr range since 1954.

Only very slight changes were evident at Earls Court in 1955, the Zephyr had now acquired the vinyl headlining as on the Zodiac, and on all three cars the rear flashing indicators were now separated from the rear sidelight units. Tubeless tyres also became part of the standard specification.

Production of the range ceased in February 1956 upon the announcement of the considerably larger Mk2 Consul/Zephyr/Zodiac range.

Datapanel: Ford Consul/Zephyr Six/Zephyr Zodiac

	Consul	Zephyr Six (Zodiac)
Engine	4 cyl, ohv	6 cyl, ohv
Capacity	1508cc	2262cc
Bore	79.3mm	79.3mm
Stroke	76.2mm	76.2mm
Compression ratio	6.8:1	6.8:1 (7.5:1)
Max BHP	47 @ 4400rpm	68 @ 4000rpm
		(71 @ 4200rpm)
Max torque	72lbs/ft @ 2300rpm	108 @ 2000rpm
		(112 @ 2000rpm)
Gearing	15.3mph/1000rpm	16.1mph/1000rpm
Tyres	5.90 x 13	6.40 x 13
Kerb weight	21.75cwt	23.5cwt (23.75cwt)
Overall length	13ft 10 1/4in	14ft 3 1/2in
Overall width	5ft 4in	5ft 4in
Wheelbase	8ft 4in	8ft 8in

Performance

	"The Autocar" 22nd July 1955	"The Autocar" 16th July 1954
Max speed:		
Top gear	73mph (mean)	80.2mph (mean)
	74mph (best)	84mph (best)
2nd gear	49mph	57mph
1st gear	29mph	31mph
Acceleration:		
0-30mph	6.9 seconds	5.4 seconds
0-50mph	17.2 seconds	13.5 seconds
0-60mph	25.9 seconds	20.4 seconds
0-70mph	–	29.7 seconds
	Top gear/2nd gear	Top gear/2nd gear
20-40mph	12.1/7.3 seconds	8.5/5.6 seconds
30-50mph	14.5/– seconds	9.6/7.9 seconds
40-60mph	17.8/– seconds	11.8/– seconds
50-70mph	–/– seconds	15.3/– seconds
Fuel consumption	29mpg (420 miles)	23.7mpg (309 miles)

Following the successful launch of their revolutionary Consul/Zephyr range in 1950, the Ford Motor Co. turned its attentions to the development of up to date replacements for their still basically pre-war style Anglia and Prefect models.

Announced in September 1953, the new Anglia (2 door) and Prefect (4 door) models – designated 100E – represented a considerable advance in almost every respect by comparison with the cars which had hitherto carried these well respected Ford names. A completely new bodyshell had been evolved. This body, whilst resembling a rather crisp, scaled down Consul, had in fact been designed from scratch around the smaller dimensions necessary for the economy end of the market.

The steel floorpan was braced by both longitudinal and transverse U-section chassis members welded into its underside, the longitudinal members continuing at the front end along the lower edge of the inner wing panels. A substantial front scuttle/bulkhead structure swept forward into the engine bay on each side to form the front suspension upper mounting points. The wide bonnet top was hinged at its forward edge, and when opened revealed a usefully wide engine bay which provided excellent accessibility for routine maintenance.

At the rear, the full-width square-shaped boot housed a 7 gallon fuel tank inside the nearside wing: its filler cap being situated on top of the bodywork aft of the rear quarter pillar. The spare wheel was carried horizontally on the offside of the compartment floor, a position which, whilst not obstructing the useful width of this compartment, would nevertheless be inconvenient should a puncture

A double-page spread in the motoring press announced the arrival of the new 100E models at prices which seem ludicrously low in relation to today's inflated pound.

The *NEW* ANGLIA

£360 PLUS P.T. £151 . 2 . (

£395 PLUS P.T. £165 . 14 . 2

The *NEW* PREFECT

Announcing in the

the first light cars

'5-Star' Class

Ford '5-Star' Motoring

The Best at lowest cost

THERE IS A FORD DEALER AT YOUR SERVICE IN YOUR TOWN

Opposite. The Anglia (top) and Prefect pictured are both pre-1957 facelift models. The 100E's sidevalve engine was a tough and durable unit and had been well-proven in earlier Ford models. Owners in search of a little more performance made the Aquaplane alloy cylinder head (lower engine picture) and twin carburettor conversion a popular 'bolt-on' accessory in the 'fifties.

occur when a large amount of luggage was being carried. Access to the boot was by a counterbalanced lid which did not extend to the boot floor level, leaving a rather high sill over which baggage had to be lifted.

Within the obvious limits imposed by an overall length and width of 12ft 7in x 5ft 0½in, coupled with a wheelbase which at 7ft 3in resulted in some rear wheelarch intrusion into the passenger space, the new Anglia and Prefect offered comfortably roomy accommodation for four people. On the Anglia, access to the rear seats was only convenient on the nearside, where the front passenger seat could be tipped forward; this facility not being provided on the driver's side of the car.

Both cars featured a moulded rubber floor covering, cloth roof lining, and pvc upholstery, with the door trims and side panels also being finished in pvc. Window winding mechanism was provided on the front doors only in the case of the Prefect, the rear doors of which were fitted with windows of the counterbalance drop type. Noticeable economies on the Anglia – which was the basic model – were the provision of only one windscreen wiper, one sunvisor, and no interior light. A usefully deep parcel shelf ran the full width of the car beneath a simple facia, and a small binnacle on the steering column housed the speedometer, fuel gauge, ammeter and an engine temperature gauge on the Prefect. Self-cancelling flashing indicators were making their first appearance on a small car, and the Prefect was unique amongst small cars in featuring a chromed horn ring on the steering wheel. Apart from the obvious two door/four door arrangement, other exterior differences were evident. In keeping with its basic image the Anglia sported a simple, silver painted three bar grille, and silver painted bumpers with just a narrow chromium strip. Both cars featured chromed door handles and hubcaps – the latter items being in fact those of the Consul/Zephyr models – the Prefect also had a chromed surround to its own distinguishing grille, and chromed bonnet motif and headlamp surrounds.

Below. An historic photograph. This is the 100E production line showing clearly that the Ford Popular 103E was built on the same lines.

Although of the sidevalve type, and with the very familiar capacity of 1172cc, the 100E engine was in fact almost entirely new; sharing only the bore and stroke (63.5mm x 92.5mm) dimensions with the previous Ford 10hp units. New features included adjustable tappets, improved valve cooling and a water pump. A new crankshaft – still running in three main bearings – was appreciably stiffer than before, largely due to an increase in main and big end bearing journal diameter. A link with the past however was the continued use of connecting rods and caps with white metalled big ends, rather than renewable shell bearings. With its single Solex carburettor, and on a compression ratio of 7.0:1, the 100E engine produced 36bhp at 4500rpm, with an equally useful 54lbs/ft torque being available at 2500rpm, figures which suggested a lively performance despite the fact that with kerb weights of $15\frac{1}{4}$ and $15\frac{1}{2}$ cwt respectively, the Anglia and Prefect were a little on the heavy side by small car standards.

A hydraulically operated clutch and an open propeller shaft were new features on a small Ford, but the three-speed gearbox controlled by a long floor-mounted lever, and with an appreciable gap between the upper two ratios was a familiar small Ford feature, as was the spiral bevel rear axle assembly. An axle ratio of 4.429:1 gave useful overall gearing of 14.6mph per 1000rpm in conjunction with 5.20 x 13 tyres. A 12 volt electrical system was most welcome on a small Ford, but a disappointment was the continued use of vacuum operated windscreen wipers without the benefit of a booster pump.

The MacPherson strut independent front suspension, Burman worm and peg steering gear, longitudinally mounted semi elliptic rear springs, and Girling all hydraulic braking system all followed very closely the layout pioneered so successfully three years earlier on the Consul/Zephyr range, although the choice of brake drums of only 7 inches diameter in this case was rather surprising in view of the obvious performance potential.

Priced at £511 and £560, the new Anglia and Prefect were slightly undercutting the Morris Minor Series II which was then being offered at £529 and £574 in two or four door form.

With a maximum speed of 70mph being accompanied by acceleration from rest to 60mph in around 30 seconds, the 100E models were introducing new levels of performance to the lower end of the market. The good low and mid range pulling power of the 1172cc engine resulted in the excellent top gear acceleration times from 20-40mph and 30-50mph of 13 seconds and 15 seconds, the latter figure being particularly useful in view of a three-speed gearbox in which the middle ratio really only allowed a comfortable 35 to 40mph. Riding characteristics and general handling qualities were also setting high standards for this class of car, but in the not unimportant matter of fuel consumption the overall 31/32mpg which most owners would achieve was rather heavy in comparison with the figures obtained by the most obvious rivals.

Swivelling front quarter windows were introduced into the specification soon after production was under way, and in October 1954 the Anglia received the chrome window surrounds, twin windscreen wipers, and the interior light, whilst the Prefect was now provided with window winding mechanism in the rear doors. 8 inch diameter brake drums were phased in early in 1955, a change which now brought the braking performance much more in line with the

This proves that you can get five people in a Prefect – even if you have to take the doors off to do it!

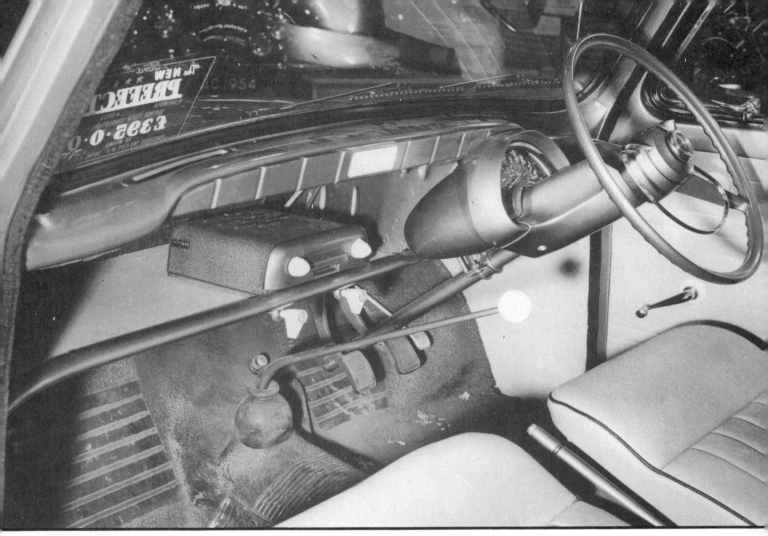

speed potential. Although not being offered by the Ford Motor Company, overdrives suitable for the 100E models were available from two independent manufacturers. Vehicle Developments of London were offering their vacuum diaphragm operated Handa overdrive unit, and this was later followed by the Murray overdrive which was mechanically operated by an additional lever sprouting from the transmission tunnel. With either of these units installed the Anglia and Prefect had a versatility of performance which could not be matched elsewhere in the small car class. Overdrive second successfully bridged the gap between direct second and top gears, whilst in overdrive top the 100E now offered an easy 65mph cruise or, alternatively, a substantial fuel saving at the model's more normal 50mph cruising gait.

De-Luxe versions became available in October 1955, recognizable externally by the addition of full length chrome strips along the waistline and twin wing mirrors. The De-Luxe interior appointments included an improved facia panel housing two circular instruments in front of the driver, ivory finish for the control knobs, strap type door pulls, and a useful increase in the front seat adjustment. Priced at £542 and £596 – to which another £12 still had to be added if a heater was specified – the De-Luxe versions seemed rather better value than the basic models which were continuing at their original price, and this despite some de-chroming which now resulted in a somewhat spartan appearance.

Announced at the same time were the Escort and Squire,

The Squire and Escort estate cars appeared in October 1955, and were equipped to the same standard as the De Luxe saloons. The Squire is replete with "Shooting Brake" style woodwork.

Two New Ford Cars!

SQUIRE   ESCORT

SEE YOUR FORD DEALER NOW!

Ford

'5-STAR' MOTORING
THE BEST AT LOWEST COST

A page from the contemporary sales brochure extolling the virtues of the Popular.

The Popular is nippy and nimble in the heaviest town traffic. All-round visibility is excellent—you'll notice the wide, deep side windows and generously large rear window that allows a wonderful view, makes parking simple. And there's a flexible gearbox that is quickly responsive, light steering, a small turning circle of only 34½ feet—it all combines to make the rush hour jungle a far less intimidating prospect, reduces driver fatigue. There's not an easier car to take shopping, or to the office. Thanks to its sensible size, large glass area and wonderful manoeuvrability, you can coax the Popular into the meanest parking space. For sheer good looks the Popular's a credit to anyone. Clean lines, good proportions, and the few discreet styling touches that make all the difference: chromed bumpers and (de luxe model) chromed front grille, sleek headlamp unit, smart twin tail light assembly. You'll win admiring glances everywhere!

estate car variations of the Anglia and Prefect. These newcomers featured rear end bodywork based closely on the 5cwt van derivative of the model which had already made its appearance, the van doors however gave way to a split horizontal tailgate. The interior trim was to De-Luxe specification in both cases, and the Squire was additionally equipped with sliding mechanism for the rear side windows; and decorative timber side strips with which to give its appearance just a hint of the "shooting brakes" of the past. Slightly stiffer rear springs and 5.60 x 13 tyres of 6 ply construction took care of the extra load capability, but provided a somewhat harsher ride in the unladen state. With prices of £587 and £631, the Escort and Squire were well placed alongside the Morris Minor Traveller at £598 and £622 in standard or De-Luxe configuration.

The earlier Ford 1172cc units had earned an enviable reputation for rugged reliability, and had been popular amongst builders of trials specials. The 100E unit continued to build upon this reputation, and the owner who wished for more peformance than standard soon had a choice of tuning kits from which to choose. Twin SU carburettor set ups were offered by several specialists, including Aquaplane Speed Equipment who could also supply a light alloy cylinder head conversion. Winning the small car category in the tough East African Safari Rally in 1956 amply underlined the durability of the standard model Anglia.

Anglia working hard at Hants & Berks 1st Autocross held at Farley Hill in 1954. (Courtesy National Motor Museum, Beaulieu).

During 1957 the Prefect lost its distinguishing winged bonnet motif when the whole range acquired a flush fitting V-shaped adornment. In October that year the 100E models underwent an extensive facelifting operation designed to keep them in the forefront of small car sales in Britain whilst development of the eventual ohv-engined replacement cars was underway. The updated 100E models were recognizable externally by an enlarged rear window of 25% greater glass area than before, a much appreciated change which gave a marked improvement in rearward vision. All models now featured chrome plated bumpers, and the De-Luxe versions had chrome inserts to the headlamp surrounds, and chrome plated grilles: that on the Anglia being of a new, mesh design. A retrograde step was that the De-Luxe specification no longer included the wing mirrors.

The interior appointments were now completely redesigned, and included a light-coloured washable headlining. The new facia

The 107E Prefect featured the new ohv engine of the all-new 105E Anglia model, and was available only in the De Luxe configuration. The V-shaped side flashes were an identifying feature of this model.

Opposite. The last of the 100E line ... The Popular which took over in September 1959, and continued as the bottom-of-the-range model until 1962.

consisted of a rectangular housing ahead of the driver containing similar instrumentation as before, and a full width parcels shelf on the basic models. A lockable glove compartment facing the passenger was a De-Luxe feature only, as was a bright metal embellishment along the recess in which were situated the various control knobs. Similar improvements were incorporated in the estate cars, however, the Squire now lost its distinctive timber decoration, this being replaced by the chromium waistline strip as on the De-Luxe saloons.

"Newtondrive" two pedal control was now available as an extra cost option at £24. This rather complicated arrangement deleted the clutch pedal, engagement of the clutch when starting from rest being by centrifugal means. A solenoid type starter switch and a vacuum servo motor controlled the clutch during gearchanging: the driver simply having to depress a switch in the gearlever knob when moving the lever. This system was available on several rival cars at the time but did not prove to be a popular option, and it was deleted from the 100E specification during the following year.

The announcement of the completely new ohv-engined 4-speed Anglia 105E model in September 1959 did not yet mean the end of the sidevalve-engined Fords. A de-trimmed version of the 100E Anglia continued in production as the new Ford Popular, with both basic and De-Luxe models on offer at £494 and £515. The basic model was indeed basic, with fixed quarter windows, plain un-patterned door trims, and devoid of the front parcel shelf, but it was the cheapest "real" car available anywhere in the world at that time and was a most thoroughly proven design. An Escort estate – approximating to the Popular De-Luxe – also remained in production.

The familiar four door Prefect now became something of a hybrid Ford, being fitted with the new Anglia ohv engine and 4-speed gearbox. Designated 107E in this configuration, the Prefect was available to De-Luxe specification only at £622, and was intended primarily to satisfy the demand for a compact four door Ford pending the arrival of the new Consul Classic in June 1961, at which time the Prefect was finally deleted. The 100E Escort was also phased out during 1961, but the Popular saloons continued until June 1962 when the last example – a De-Luxe model – left Dagenham, thus bringing to an end the 30 year era of small sidevalve-engined Fords.

Datapanel: Ford Anglia/Prefect 100E

Ford Anglia/Prefect 100E

Engine	4 cyl, sidevalve
Capacity	1172cc
Bore	63.5mm
Stroke	92.5mm
Compression ratio	7.0:1
Max BHP	36 @ 4500rpm
Max torque	54lbs/ft @ 2500rpm
Gearing	14.6mph/1000rpm
Tyres	5.20 x 13 (5.60 x 13 Estate car)
Kerb weight	15 1/4cwt (Anglia)
	15 1/2cwt (Prefect)
Overall length	12ft 7in
Overall width	5ft 0 1/2in
Wheelbase	7ft 3in

Performance

	Anglia "The Motor" Road test No. 18/54	Prefect "The Motor" Road test No. 22/57
Max speed:		
Top gear	70.2mph (mean)	70.7mph (mean)
	72.6mph (best)	70.9mph (best)
2nd gear	48mph	46mph
1st gear	27mph	24mph
Acceleration:		
0-30mph	7.0 seconds	7.1 seconds
0-50mph	18.5 seconds	20.2 seconds
0-60mph	29.4 seconds	32.2 seconds
	Top gear/2nd gear	Top gear/2nd gear
20-40mph	12.6/7.4 seconds	13.5/7.8 seconds
30-50mph	14.8/– seconds	15.4/– seconds
40-60mph	18.8/– seconds	21.3/– seconds
Fuel consumption	30.3mpg (1334 miles)	30.4mpg (1682 miles)

Chapter 3
Ford

Consul/ Zephyr/ Zodiac Mk2

By 1954, Dagenham's Consul, Zephyr and Zodiac range was firmly established as the leader in its important market sector, and development was now put in hand for the eventual replacement models.

The basic concept of the existing range was to be continued with just one important difference: the second generation cars were to be appreciably larger than the originals. Although enlarged and completely re-styled, the new bodyshells did in fact repeat almost exactly the type of construction and the design features pioneered by the MkI cars, and also, upon their introduction in February 1956 were immediately seen to once again bear a strong visual resemblance to contemporary American Fords.

A large glass area and much crisper profile characterized the new MkII models. These were very handsome cars and they created a great deal of public interest on their introduction.

Opposite, top. The rather pompous Ford caption for this publicity photograph reads: "A complete absence of extraneous projections on the new Consul leaves the eye free to enjoy the clean low silhouette which has a flow and rhythm in keeping with the highest standards of creative design. High performance with economy is provided by a new "oversquare" ohv engine of 1703cc."

Opposite, centre. Describing the new Zephyr in this photograph, Ford said: "The new Zephyr combines arresting beauty with classic simplicity. It is powered by a new "oversquare" ohv engine of 2553cc which provides vivid acceleration to high cruising and maximum speeds".

Oppposite, bottom. Elaborate tail-end styling instantly identified the Zodiac from the rear.

The *NEW* CONSUL

The *NEW* ZEPHYR

Plus *NEW* CONVERTIBLES

(The Zephyr is illustrated)

See these new cars at your Ford dealer's now!

FORD '5-STAR' MOTORING AND FORD SERVICE TOO
THE BEST AT LOWEST COST

Main picture. The Abbott Estate car conversions gave the MkII models more than just a hint of the American "Ranch Wagon" look. A 1958 Zodiac is pictured here.

Top left. A padded facia was a feature of the Low-Line cars. In the straight ahead position, the horn-ring occupied the lower half of the steering wheel.

Bottom left. The Low-Line Consul De Luxe.

Bottom, right. To many enthusiasts the ultimate MkII – a Low Line Zodiac Convertible.

With bodywork 7 inches longer and 5 inches wider than before, and on a wheelbase increased by 3 inches, the new cars were very generous six-seaters and, with a larger glass area than any previous British car, offered the occupants an uninterrupted all round view. Interior appointments now included vinyl rooflining in the Consul, although carpeting was still confined to the Zephyr and Zodiac only, with the 4-cylinder car continuing to feature a rubber floor covering. The trim specification and general equipment level was in fact almost identical to that of the previous cars with the Zodiac once again being the most comprehensively equipped: although its specification, in Mk2 form, did not include the wing mirrors and auxiliary lamps. Making an early appearance in Britain was the combined ignition/starter switch, whilst a sharp contrast was the continued use of vacuum operated windscreen wipers ...

As before, the engine compartment differed in length according to the engine installed, and three different grilles identified the cars as Consul, Zephyr, or Zodiac when viewed head on. The very wide bonnet was now counterbalanced, and when opened revealed a truly capacious engine bay which offered unusually convenient accessibility for routine maintenance. At the rear, visually balancing the roomy front end was a 20 cubic feet capacity luggage boot, with the fuel tank – now of $10\frac{1}{2}$ gallons capacity – occupying a position underneath and between the rear chassis members as on the MkI cars.

Offering such a considerable increase in accommodation had resulted in a larger frontal area and a weight penalty of around $\frac{3}{4}$cwt, factors which however were more than adequately compensated for by enlarging the cylinder capacities of the engines. An increase in the bore measurement to 82.5mm still allowed ample water circulation around each cylinder, and a completely new, slightly longer throw crankshaft was provided which gave a stroke of 79.5mm. Larger bearing journal diameters than previously compensated for the longer throw, and hollowed webs were a notable feature of this new crankshaft which as before ran in either three or four main bearings and was fully counterbalanced. As a result of these changes the total capacities were increased to 1703cc and 2553cc for the 4 and 6-cylinder units respectively.

Single Zenith carburettors were still employed, with that on the Zodiac having an oil bath air cleaner rather than the washable gauze type of the two cheaper cars. With a compression ratio of 7.8:1 the new engines produced 59bhp and 85bhp at 4400rpm in both cases, with corresponding torque outputs of 91lbs/ft at 2300rpm and 132lbs/ft at 2000rpm promising good pulling power. An increase in the clutch diameter from 8 inches to $8\frac{1}{2}$ inches was a feature of the 6-cylinder cars only, whilst apart from a new mainshaft the gearbox and its ratios remained exactly as in the previous models. The Borg Warner overdrive was to be available once again as an option on the Zephyr and Zodiac. Revised axle ratios of 4.11:1 and 3.9:1, in conjunction with the same tyre sizes as before now gave overall gearing of 16.9mph per 1000rpm and 18.5mph per 1000rpm for the Consul and Zephyr/Zodiac respectively, and a correspondingly useful increase in the range of the lower gears.

The Burman steering gear followed closely the layout of the MkI cars, but now provided a turning circle which, at around 35 feet, was a considerable improvement over the 41 feet required by the original models, whilst a slightly lower ratio in the steering box now gave unusually light control by big car standards. Also very similar to before were the MacPherson struts at the front and longitudinally mounted semi-elliptic leaf springs at the rear, with the only modifications being those necessary to accommodate the system in the larger and heavier cars. The Girling braking system once again consisted of 9 inch diameter drums all round, but with an increase in front shoe width from $1\frac{3}{4}$ inches to $2\frac{1}{2}$ inches giving a new total lining area of 147 square inches.

Under favourable conditions the Consul had now moved into the 80mph class, and would accelerate from rest to 60mph in 25 seconds. Despite the higher gearing, acceleration in top gear actually showed a slight improvement from speeds as low as 20mph and was appreciably better than the MkI Consul at the top end of the range, whilst the overtaking performance was enhanced by second gear now being usefully quicker than top up to nearly 50mph. Only a small increase in fuel consumption was evident, with around 24/25mph being an easily obtainable overall figure, and a 50mph cruise would still just return 30mpg.

The Zephyrs and Zodiacs could now reach 70mph from a standstill in 25 seconds, and continue to accelerate strongly to more than 85mph before tailing off to a maximum of 90mph. Once again top gear pulling power was really excellent, with the ability to go from 20mph right through to 70mph in this ratio in only 25 seconds indicating that high cross country averages could be attained in a particularly effortless manner. The overall fuel consumption was much the same as the MkI Zephyr at around 22/23mpg, and if the optional overdrive was specified journey averages of 30mpg were possible. The handling qualities which had played an important part in making the standard MkI Zephyr a Monte Carlo winner, were actually improved upon in the Mk2, thanks largely being due to the increase in track and a very slightly less nose heavy front/rear weight distribution. However, being slightly lower geared, the steering was not now quite so quick as before.

All of this was a combination of performance, economy, and accommodation which could not quite be matched elsewhere at the tax paid prices being asked of £781, £871, and £968. Also available from the start were a Consul and Zephyr convertible at £946 and £1036, and when the Mk2s made their first Earls Court appearance later in the year these were joined by a Zodiac convertible at £1253.

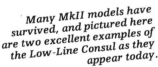

Many MkII models have survived, and pictured here are two excellent examples of the Low-Line Consul as they appear today.

Farnham estate cars were also now available from E.D. Abbott, who were taking partially built saloons from Dagenham and completing them as estate cars at their Surrey works. For an extra £187, buyers could now specify fully automatic transmission on either of the 6-cylinder cars, and, at £1058, a Zephyr equipped with this option was the cheapest automatic car available anywhere outside the United States.

Slight changes were evident on the Ford stand at Earls Court in October 1957, at which time a Consul De-Luxe was added to the range – trimmed almost to Zodiac standard, and recognizable externally by a contrasting colour applied to the roof. All three cars featured a re-designed front seat frame, foam rubber padding in addition to the seat springs, and upholstery styling changes which did away with the previously buttoned seat coverings. Apart from a completely new range of colours, the Consul and the Zodiac remained unchanged externally, whereas the Zephyr now acquired the Zodiac sidelamps in the extremities of a new grille: the design of which resembled the MkI Zephyr. Technical changes were confined to a new gearchange mechanism completely enclosed in the steering column – giving a much neater appearance – and the adoption of a Burman re-circulating ball steering box with a further slight reduction in gearing which now gave extreme lightness of control.

Priced at £818, or £871 for the De-Luxe specification, the Consul offered usefully more space and performance than both its nearest rivals – the Morris Oxford and Standard Ensign which were selling at £884 and £899 respectively. The Zephyr and Zodiac, at £916 and £1013, had a worthwhile price advantage over Vauxhall's new PA series Velox and Cresta which were offering similar accommodation and straight line performance to the big Fords for £983 and £1073. The obvious BMC rivals, the Westminster A95 and A105, were now rather highly priced in this sector at £1034 and £1235.

Whilst the performance of the standard models was more than adequate for the vast majority of buyers, those who did require more speed and acceleration were well catered for by the tuning specialists, with 4 and 6-branch exhaust manifolds, twin or triple SU carburettors and re-worked cylinder heads all being readily obtainable. At £135, a Raymond Mays conversion – once again featuring a six port light alloy cylinder head, twin SU carburettors, and a complete dual exhaust system – would enable a Zephyr to accelerate from rest to 90mph in only 25 seconds whilst on its way to a maximum of more than 100mph.

No changes were visible on the big Fords at Earls Court in 1958, although work was in progress at Dagenham on a face lift for the Mk2 which was to be announced in February 1959. A new, slightly flatter roof panel was introduced, giving the car a lower silhouette than before. Bright metal cappings in a rustless chromium alloy now completely covered the front and rear windscreen rubbers, and a capping of similar material was applied to the roof drip rail. New chrome plated headlamp hoods were rather less sharp than the earlier painted type. All three cars received individual re-designed tail light clusters, and the De-Luxe Consul now had chrome cappings along the horizontal flutes in the rear panel, new anodized aluminium wheel trims, and a grille badge. The new wheeltrims also found their way onto the Zodiac, replacing the previous chrome plated rings. The interior appointments were completely redesigned and included padded, crushable sun visors, and a full width padded facia top and instrument cowl. A new rectangular speedometer housed the fuel gauge and engine temperature gauge, the latter being in place of the ammeter of the earlier models. Beneath the instrument ran a bright metal strip containing re-designed control knobs which now featured internationally recognized symbols for identification. The seat and door trimmings were re-styled, and the basic Consul now had the doorpull/armrests as on the De-Luxe and the two 6-cylinder cars. The front swivelling quarter windows were now of a positive locking thief-proof design.

The concentric gearchange mechanism introduced late in 1957 had proved to be less accurate than before, and so now the original arrangement with the linkage running outside the steering column was re-adopted, although now with the column and change mechanism neatly shrouded. A new handbrake lever with twist grip operation was another worthwhile improvement. These considerable modifications had been introduced without any increase in price, and only two months later a purchase tax reduction in the 1959 budget brought the prices of these "low line" Mk2 models down to an extremely attractive £773, £865, and £957.

Ever since its introduction the Mk2 Zephyr had competed successfully in international rallies, and had by now several awards to its credit. These were added to in a big way in 1959 with the Zephyr taking the Team Prize in three major events, the East African Safari, the Dutch International Tulip Rally, and the Alpine Rally before going on to win outright the R.A.C. Rally of Gt Britain in November. Success also came in saloon car racing that year, with Jeff Uren winning the BRSCC Saloon Car Championship in his Raymond Mays modified Zephyr.

Since as early as 1958, in those international events in which modifications to the competing cars were permitted, some of the "works" rally Zephyrs had featured disc brakes on the front wheels. In September 1960 this arrangement was introduced on the production models – including the Consul which now became the cheapest disc braked car in the world – as an extra cost option at £29. Servo assistance was provided, and the system included a vacuum reservoir which ensured continued assistance should the engine stall. A conversion kit, at £32 plus a fitting charge, was also made available for those owners who wished to modify an existing car. The popularity of the disc brake option was such that this equipment was absorbed into the standard specification in June 1961, with an appropriate increase in the basic price. Sealed beam headlamps were introduced at the same time, and these later model Mk2s could be recognized by the deletion of the name script from the upper rear wings.

The Consul now became known as the Consul 375, with this script actually appearing on the boot lid. The number 375 did not have any technical significance, being introduced purely to distinguish the large 4-cylinder car during its final months of production from the completely new ranges of smaller Fords which were scheduled for introduction in 1961 and 1962, and which were to have the benefit of the well respected Consul name as a prefix to their full titles – the Consul Classic 315 being the first example of this theme.

Production of the Mk2 range ceased in April 1962 with the introduction of the futuristically styled Mk3 models, of which the 4-cylinder car now became known as the Zephyr 4, with a Zephyr 6 and Zodiac completing the line up.

Datapanel: Ford Consul/Zephyr/Zodiac MKII

	Consul	Zephyr/Zodiac
Engine	4 cyl, ohv	6 cyl, ohv
Capacity	1703cc	2553cc
Bore	82.5mm	82.5mm
Stroke	79.5mm	79.5mm
Compression ratio	7.8:1	7.8:1
Max BHP	59 @ 4400rpm	85 @ 4400rpm
Max torque	91lbs/ft @ 2300rpm	132lbs/ft @ 2000rpm
Gearing	16.9mph/1000rpm	18.5mph/1000rpm
Tyres	5.90 x 13	6.40 x 13
Kerb weight	22.25cwt	24.5cwt
Overall length	14ft 4in (14ft 7in "Low Line")	14ft 10 1/2in (15ft 1/2in Zodiac)
Overall width	5ft 9in	5ft 9in
Wheelbase	8ft 8in	8ft 11in

Performance

	"The Motor" RT No. 2/58	"The Motor" RT No. 9/56
Max speed:		
Top gear	78.1mph (mean)	87.9mph (mean)
	79.6mph (best)	90.5mph (best)
2nd gear	60mph	62mph
1st gear	34mph	36mph
Acceleration:		
0-30mph	6.4 seconds	4.6 seconds
0-50mph	16.0 seconds	11.3 seconds
0-60mph	24.2 seconds	17.1 seconds
0-70mph	38.2 seconds	24.3 seconds
0-80mph	–	37.8 seconds
	Top gear/2nd gear	Top gear/2nd gear
20-40mph	11.8/7.7 seconds	8.0/5.2 seconds
30-50mph	12.7/9.2 seconds	8.4/6.2 seconds
40-60mph	15.6/17.3 seconds	10.1/10.0 seconds
50-70mph	23.0/– seconds	12.9/– seconds
60-80mph	–/–	20.7/– seconds
Fuel consumption	24.7mpg (1547 miles)	21.5mpg (1553 miles)

Chapter 4
Hillman

Minx
MkIII-VIII

A "MkI" Minx, which was basically the 1940 model – the first monocoque Minx – quickly appeared after the war, and was followed by a slightly restyled Mk2 in December 1947.

Meanwhile, development work on a completely new bodyshell was taking place, and the result of this was the appearance of the Minx MkIII in September 1948. The new four door body was braced by full length box section members welded into the floor on each side, and also utilised the partially boxed-in sills as additional stiffening members. A large glass area was a notable feature, with a full width curved windscreen making an early appearance on an inexpensive British car. Combined head and sidelamp units were styled into the front wings, which themselves were styled to continue rearwards to meet the leading edge of the rear wing, the forward outer section of which was formed by the rear door outer skin. Rather narrow section chrome plated bumpers protected each end of the car, and a chromium finish was also applied to the simple low set grille of horizontal bars, the lamp surrounds, external boot lid hinges, door handles and quarter window frames and hubcaps. Overall, with its remarkably smooth styling and discreet ornamentation, in its appearance the MkIII Minx was a generation or so ahead of the similar sized opposition in 1948.

The wide, rear hinged bonnet gave good accessibility, but was not self-supporting having to be propped open with a stay. The full-width boot lid was fitted with a self-supporting strut, and when open gave access to a roomy compartment beneath the steel floor of which was a separate stowage space for the spare wheel. Alongside this, in the nearside, was situated a 7½ gallon fuel tank. All four passenger

A 1949 advertisement for the new MkIII Minx, one of the earliest postwar models to offer full-width bodywork. Like many others of the time, the ad makes reference to the export drive which was essential to Britain at the time.

Friend of the family . . .

There never was a car which made friends as quickly as the Minx.   In use throughout the world, always the leader in its class, the Hillman Minx is roomy, comfortable, economical and thoroughly dependable.   Big car comfort, independent front suspension, Synchromatic finger-tip gear control, Lockheed Hydraulic brakes, and the proved reliable Hillman Minx engine, are features which are attracting a host of new friends in countries overseas, and which will ensure the lasting popularity of the Minx at home when the great domestic demand can be more fully met.

The HILLMAN MINX MAGNIFICENT

SALOON — CONVERTIBLE COUPE — ESTATE CAR

doors were equipped with window winding mechanism, and both front and rear seats were upholstered in pleated cloth with leather edging. In what was quite a compact car, with a wheelbase of only 7 feet 9 inches, the rear seat was, inevitably, almost over the rear axle line; and the intrusion of the rear wheel arches dictated only two occupants in the rear. The front bench seat was slightly wider, but the Minx was not really intended to be anything other than a comfortable four seater model.

The floor was carpeted, and facing the driver was a sprung T-spoked steering wheel. The facia featured a central instrument panel with a large circular speedometer offset to the driver's side. Other instrumentation was confined to a fuel gauge alongside which was a matching recess into which the optionally available electric clock would be fitted if specified. Twin windscreen wipers, and semaphore indicators were a standard feature, but there was a sunvisor on the driver's side only.

The mechanical specification included the well-tried sidevalve engine of the earlier Minx models, but which was now nearing the end of its development potential. Improvements in this latest installation were confined to hardened steel seat inserts for the exhaust valves, and a new four-bladed fan. With its bore and stroke of 63mm x 95mm giving a capacity of 1185cc, a single Solex carburettor and a compression ratio of 6.3:1, the engine produced 35bhp at 4100rpm. The four-speed gearbox was also substantially that of the previous model, its ratios selected by a column-mounted lever, and featuring rather low indirect ratios; the lowest of which was unsynchronised. An open propeller shaft and a spiral bevel final drive unit with a ratio of 5.22:1 completed the transmission, giving overall gearing of 14.2mph per 1000rpm.

Independent front suspension units consisting of wishbones and coil springs were mounted on a substantial crossmember, and so formed a separate sub-assembly. The engine was also mounted to this crossmember prior to installation in the car: the combined assembly then being offered up to the body from beneath as one of the final assembly line operations. Burman worm and nut steering gear completed the front end arrangements, whilst at the rear were half-elliptic leaf springs attached longitudinally to the box section crossmembers of the lower bodywork. A transverse anti-roll bar was also situated at the rear. The all hydraulic braking system was by Lockheed, and consisted of 8 inch diameter drums and a total lining area of 92 square inches. The roadwheels were 16 inches in diameter and fitted with 5.00 section tyres.

Priced at £505, the Minx was rather more expensive than its two most obvious four-seater rivals, the Austin Devon at £463 and the Vauxhall Wyvern at £447. With a maximum speed of 65mph and acceleration from rest to 60mph in around 46 seconds the Minx was offering a broadly similar performance to these rival cars, fuel economy also was similar, being just on the right side of 30mpg at a 50mph cruising speed. However, for the extra cost, the Minx buyer was getting an appreciably more modern looking car which would obviously be in production in substantially similar form for some considerable time ahead.

A Minx Estate Car was announced at the same time, priced at £594 and differing noticeably in appearance from the saloon. Although the same windscreen was fitted, the roof line of the estate car was 5 inches higher and continued almost horizontally to a squared-up and slightly longer back end. Only the two front passenger doors were fitted, with the estate car section featuring almost full length sliding side windows. Two rear doors opened outwards from the centre. Separate front seats were fitted, and in usual estate car fashion the rear seat squab could be folded forward.

A two door convertible followed early in 1949, priced at £575, and in December that year the Minx was re-designated MkIV upon the announcement of a larger capacity – 1265cc – engine. Although still of the sidevalve type, the new power unit was considerably more than just a larger-bored version of the original

The Minx became the MkIV late in 1949 with the introduction of a larger engine.

MORE POWER TO THE MINX!

WITH ITS NEW FULLY PROVED PLUS-POWER ENGINE
the MINX MAGNIFICENT ... a full size family car
famous for its economy, gives you

MORE *Speed* AT THE GETAWAY
.... from a standing start to 50 m.p.h in 21·3 seconds

MORE *Power* ON THE HILLS
... climbs steep gradients with a full load in top gear

YET RUNNING COSTS ARE AS LOW AS EVER!

The MkV model was identifiable externally by virtue of the chromium strip along the side, and the vertical end pieces for the grille. The drawing in this period advertisement is rather more accurate than that in the preceding illustration although the three occupants of the front bench seat must be remarkably small!

MORE HEADROOM · MORE SAFETY · MORE STYLE

The latest Hillman Minx gives you even more value. New features include more headroom, double-dipping headlamps, lighter steering and weather-proofed brake drums. Refinements in styling—with highly attractive colour schemes—are added to outstanding Minx performance and economy to complete 20 years of continuous development.

You get still more in the *LATEST* Minx—

...*and you get still more out of it!*

THE HILLMAN MINX

SALOON · CONVERTIBLE COUPE · ESTATE CAR

Craftsman Built by the Rootes Group

Two recent photographs of a MkV convertible which is in original condition, except for a new hood. A usefully large rear window is a good feature of this convertible top.

engine, in fact being built around an entirely new block with wider – 65 mm – bores and improved water circulation. Engine cooling was also now assisted by a water pump. The stroke remained the same at 95mm, but in the interests of smoother running at high rpm a new fully counterbalanced crankshaft was fitted. These changes, in conjunction with an increase in compression ratio to 6.6:1 resulted in 37.5bhp now being available at 4200rpm, a small but useful increase which brought the 0 to 60mph time down to 40 seconds and allowed the Minx to nudge the 70mph mark. Slightly more rounded section bumpers, and separate sidelights were the only external MkIV identification features, whilst inside the Minx now had plastic upholstery.

Several modifications were phased-in during 1951, including, in the engine, modified pistons which were tin-plated for longer life and an improved oil strainer fitted to the oil pump intake. The cooling system pressure was raised from 4 to 7lbs/sq.in. A new Burman worm and peg steering box was introduced, giving more accurate and slightly higher geared steering than previously. Inside the car, in the interests of increased headroom, the front bench seat was lowered by 1 inch.

From October 1951 these improved cars were designated MkV, and were now identified as such by a new chrome strip along the front wing and door, vertical chrome ends to the radiator grille, and stainless steel stone-guards on the leading edge of the rear wing. The convertible was now provided with a cloth tonneau cover, and the massive purchase tax increases earlier in the year had been largely responsible for prices now of £701 and £825 for the saloon and drophead models, respectively.

February 1953 was the 21st anniversary of the first Hillman Minx, and this was celebrated by the introduction of the MkVI "Anniversary" Minx. The changes in fact were few, but the MkVI was recognizable by a new bonnet top, giving a slightly lower line, and a new grille with an almost oval, broad chromium surround. An

The MkVI "Anniversary" Minx was the first with the lower bonnet line, and the last with the short tail-end. This is another preserved car.

Opposite, top. The MkVII introduced the longer boot and more balanced appearance. The Whitewall tyres, wheeltrim rings, and overriders were all optional extras.

important addition to the range was announced at the same time, the Minx Californian. Based on the two door convertible body, the Californian was an attractive hardtop model with a fully wrap-round three piece rear window. Pillarless side windows could be wound down completely out of sight and the Californian came in dual tone colour schemes.

The MKVI was in fact short lived, and on the Hillman stand at Earls Court in October 1953 the MKVII was on display. The principle change was now extended rear bodywork lengthening the car by 2 inches overall and giving a small increase in luggage space. A larger rear window was also new, whilst the front screen now featured a chrome surround. The braking system was modified slightly by the adoption of slightly larger hydraulic cylinders in the front drums, and improved brake linings of the moulded type replaced the previously woven linings. Wheeltrim rings and whitewall tyres were now listed as optional extras, and purchase tax reductions had resulted in prices now of £666 for the saloon, £723 for the convertible and Californian; and £766 for the Minx estate car.

The MkVII models continued for just one year, and in October 1954 the range went into MKVIII configuration with the announcement of a completely new overhead valve engine. The new engine was of "square" dimensions, both the bore and stroke being 76.2mm giving a total capacity of 1390cc. The crankshaft ran in three main bearings and was of a particularly sturdy design: the main bearing journal diameters of $2\frac{1}{4}$ inches suggesting that it could handle an increased capacity at a later date. The cylinder head featured separate ports, and the overhead valves were pushrod operated. With a single Zenith carburettor and a compression ratio of 7.0:1 the new unit produced 43bhp at 4400rpm, and whilst the gearbox ratios remained unchanged the opportunity was taken to raise the overall gearing to 15.3mph per 1000rpm by the adoption of a 4.778:1 axle ratio. Tyre sizes were now changed to 5.60 x 15.

The new engine weighed slightly more than its predecessors, and in view of this the anti-roll bar was re-located to the front on the ohv cars. These modifications endowed the Minx with an almost 75mph capability, markedly improved acceleration and a small but useful improvement in the steady speed fuel economy. The ohv saloon also featured minor trim improvements, including a new steering wheel with a full circle horn ring and a passenger's sunvisor. It was designated Minx MkVIII De-Luxe and priced at £681. The convertible and Californian models also received the new engine but the estate car, and a somewhat de-trimmed saloon which was to be known as the Minx Special – at £649 – continued with the sidevalve unit. All the latest cars were now distinguishable at the front by a new grille of close set vertical bars.

The range was also now extended by the addition of the Hillman Husky. On a wheelbase shorter by 9 inches, the Husky was based on the Minx Special saloon ahead of the centre pillar, rearwards of which, however, was a very short estate car-type body differing from the Minx estate not only in respect of its reduced length, but also in the fact that it had a single rear door and followed the saloon's lower roof line. The power unit was a de-tuned (35bhp) version of the 1265cc sidevalve engine, and at a price of £564 the Husky was a very attractive compact four seater "all purpose" type of vehicle.

Opposite, bottom. The Hillman Californian offered a touch of glamour for just £723.

Inset. Excellent visibility rearwards was a useful Californian feature.

The Minx MkVIII De Luxe model was the first with the new ohv engine.

With ohv performance, the MkVIII Minx Convertible was a very attractive proposition.

The sidevalve engine was retained in the MkVIII Minx Special which was simply a basic equipment model.

88

HILLMAN

.. leaders in looks
.. in luxury
.. in low cost performance

Minx O.H.V. de Luxe Saloon —
the luxury light car, now available
in two-tone colour schemes.

Choose *just* the car for you! Five gleaming, elegant value-for-money models with the widest-ever choice of tasteful and exciting colours. Good looks, exceptional comfort, safety and economy *plus* an exhilarating o.h.v. engine that's a pleasure to drive.

MINX DE LUXE SALOON · MINX SPECIAL SALOON
MINX CONVERTIBLE · CALIFORNIAN · ESTATE CAR

Two-tone paintwork became available in October 1955, at which time the range was re-designated MkVIIIA. This is a contemporary advertisement.

The short-wheelbase utility Husky model was also powered by the sidevalve engine, and shared many other features with the Minx Special saloon.

The Minx Special and Minx Estate acquired the ohv engine in October 1955, at which time the Minx De-Luxe saloon received a full-length chrome strip along the side as the division of new two-tone "Gay Look" colour schemes. The "Gay Look" could be specified on the convertible and Californian models too, and in this configuration the cars were designated MkVIIIA. The Husky continued unchanged, and in fact remained in production as a separate model in its own right long after the MkVIII models had been deleted in May 1956 upon the announcement of the completely re-bodied "New Minx" Series 1.

Datapanel: Hillman Minx MkIII to VIII

	MkIII to VII	MkVIII
Engine	4 cyl, Sidevalve	4 cyl, ohv
Capacity	1185cc (1265cc MkIV to VII)	1390cc
Bore	63mm (65mm MkIV to VII)	76.2mm
Stroke	95mm	76.2mm
Compression ratio	6.3:1 (6.6:1 MkIV to VII)	7.0:1
Max BHP	35 @ 4100rpm 37.5 @ 4200rpm (MkIV to VII)	43 @ 4400rpm
Gearing	14.3mph/1000rpm	15.3mph/1000rpm
Tyres	5.00 x 16	5.60 x 15
Kerb weight	18 3/4cwt	19 3/4cwt
Overall length	13ft 1 1/4in (13fr 3 1/4in MkVII)	13ft 3 1/4in
Overall width	5ft 2in	5ft 2in
Wheelbase	7ft 9in	7ft 9in

Performance

	"The Autocar" December 2nd 1949 MkIV 1265cc	"The Motor" RT No. 6/55
Max speed:		
Top gear	67mph (mean)	73.8mph (mean) 76.9mph (best)
3rd gear	52mph	60mph
2nd gear	32mph	36mph
1st gear	21mph	Not recorded
Acceleration:		
0-30mph	8.9 seconds	6.7 seconds
0-50mph	23.9 seconds	13.3 seconds
0-60mph	40.2 seconds	29.2 seconds
	Top gear/3rd gear	Top gear/3rd gear
20-40mph	13.8/9.6 seconds	13.0/8.9 seconds
30-50mph	16.8/13.9 seconds	14.7/11.1 seconds
40-60mph	–/–	20.3/– seconds
Fuel consumption	30-37mpg	29.5mpg (1389 miles)

Although only 1 inch longer overall, and actually reduced in outside width by $2\frac{3}{4}$ inches, the "New Minx" Series 1 offered usefully more interior space for its four occupants than did the superseded model. A wheelbase longer by 3 inches – now 8ft – allowed the rear seat to be mounted a little further ahead of the axle line whilst still giving $1\frac{1}{2}$ inches more knee room in the rear compartment. The bodywork was slightly more "full width" in its styling features; and this allowed a 2 inch increase in the width of the front bench seat. Although the ground clearance remained the same the new model was lower overall, and headroom was reduced by 2 inches. Wider doors both front and rear made entry and exit easier, particularly to, and from, the rear compartment where there was now less wheel-arch intrusion. The bodyshell was in fact an appropriately modified version of that of the two door pillarless hardtop Sunbeam Rapier which had been announced the previous October, and which was of course manufactured by the same group of companies.

Longitudinal stiffeners on each side were employed in the lower regions, but not now running the entire length as in the previous Minx. Instead, front and rear stiffeners now terminated where they met with transverse stiffening members, the outer ends of which themselves were welded into the body sills. At the rear, the new Minx offered more luggage space than before, although the spare wheel was now mounted in an upright position in the offside of the luggage compartment. Clips were provided to secure the jack and wheelbrace in position behind the wheel. A $7\frac{1}{4}$ gallon capacity fuel tank was beneath the boot floor, with its filler tube protruding conveniently out of the back panel which ran beneath the boot lid. The boot lid itself was now counterbalanced as was the wide, rear-hinged bonnet top. The De-Luxe model featured chrome plated headlamp hoods, although chrome plating generally was once again quite discreet; leaving room for further embellishments if necessary for future "face lifted" models.

The large glass area included a fully wrap-round rear screen, giving a light and spacious effect to the interior. The bench seats, roof lining and lower sections of the door trims were covered in Vynide, with a strip of narrow, ribbed nylon cloth running across the door trims beneath the window sill. All the doors were equipped with window winders, with swivelling quarter windows also being a feature in the front. The doors, and the seats were devoid of armrests. Carpeting covered the floor on the De-Luxe model, and included sensibly sized rubber heel pads in the front compartment. Rubber floorcovering was fitted throughout in the Minx Special, which also had a cheaper plastic upholstery material. A two-spoked steering wheel – complete with a full horn ring on the De-Luxe car – faced the driver, and there was a usefully deep parcel shelf on each side of a central instrument panel which housed three circular dials. A large speedometer in the centre was flanked by a fuel gauge and engine temperature gauge. Mounted in a small binnacle on the steering column shroud were warning lights for ignition and low oil pressure.

The power unit was an uprated version of the 1390cc ohv engine. Combustion chambers of reduced depth in an otherwise similar cylinder head as before raised the compression ratio to 8.0:1 which resulted in an increased power output of 47.5bhp at 4600rpm. The indirect gear ratios, the axle ratio and wheel and tyre sizes remained as before, again resulting in overall gearing of 15.3mph per

The luggage compartment of the new model was very conveniently shaped and capacious.

Looking somewhat larger-than-life in this 1956 advertisement, the new Minx was, in fact, only 1 inch longer than its predecessor. It did, however, provide usefully more interior space. The Hillman advertisements of this period seem to major on performance with economy or quality of build.

1000rpm. The master cylinders for the hydraulic clutch and Lockheed braking system were now operated by pendant pedals, but in other respects the clutch and brakes were as before. The coil and wishbone independent front suspension units were attached to a fabricated hollow steel crossmember which was bolted to the body. An anti-roll bar was attached to the forward pressings of the lower wishbone. The rear leaf springs now featured an adverse camber. The layout of the Burman steering gear differed from the previous Minx with the centre track rod of the three piece track rod arrangement running behind the engine block.

A two door convertible was announced simultaneously, but as the Rootes Group were already producing a similarly bodied two door hardtop model, the Sunbeam Rapier, there was to be no Californian model in the new Minx range. The new, lower lines resulted in a particularly smart convertible, and the plastic coated fabric hood featured an unusually large rear window for this type of top. Access to the rear compartment was relatively easy due to the folding arrangements of the split front seat squab, and the trim level of the convertible approximated to that of the De-Luxe saloon car. With prices of £748, £773, and £848 for the Special, De-Luxe, and the convertible, respectively, the new Minx series was very well placed, with just one rival model offering a very similar accommodation and performance level, this being the Austin A50 Cambridge at £772 and £820 in its basic and De-Luxe specification.

A well-kept Jubilee Minx is pictured here at a recent classic car gathering.

TO COMMEMORATE 50 YEARS OF

HILLMAN
AND 25 YEARS OF
MINX

£529 plus p.t. £265.17.0.
White-wall tyres, chromium rimfinishers, over-riders available as extras.

ROOTES PRESENT THE
NEW *Jubilee* MINX
EVEN MORE — REFINEMENTS — EVEN GREATER PERFORMANCE

A restyled grille identified the new Jubilee Minx. The model designation was now Series II.

On the road, the new Minx showed a useful improvement in almost every respect over the previous Minx MkVIII. A maximum speed of around 77/78mph was accompanied by the ability to reach 60mph from rest in 27 seconds. Quite hard driving would still return more than 30mpg, and nearer 40mpg could be obtained in steady open road cruising conditions.

An estate car model appeared in June 1957, which, unlike the earlier Minx estates, featured the saloon's low roof line and was equipped with four passenger doors: the rears having squared up window frames. The tailgate was split horizontally at window level. The rear seat could of course be folded flat, and behind this was a false floor at the same height as the folded squab. Beneath the false floor was the normal saloon boot floor pressing, and here the spare wheel resided horizontally; being accessible by simply removing the false floor. With the upper floor removed, the spare wheel could of course then be mounted vertically in the wheel well as in the saloon, thus giving a much deeper, although narrower and shorter loading space. Extra leaves in the rear springs took care of the extra loads possible, and an axle ratio of 5.22:1 lowered the overall gearing to 14.3mph:1000rpm.

For those motorists who found the compact dimensions and well finished trimmings of the Minx exactly to their taste but wished for something usefully quicker, tuning specialists Alexander Engineering Co. Ltd., were offering an interesting performance package deal which met with the full approval of the Rootes Group. For an additional cost of £172, Alexander could provide a Minx with a reworked cylinder head, twin SU carburettors, a floor gearchange/Laycock overdrive and a re-calibrated speedometer. The Alexander Minx was identified by a "flash" of second colour running the length of the car and also by Alexander badges on the front wings. These modifications put the Minx into the genuine 90mph category and, as the twin carburettors encroached into the battery space, the battery was removed to the luggage boot with the resulting change in weight distribution being said to have a beneficial effect on the already pleasant handling qualities of this model.

1957 was the 25th anniversary of the introduction of the first Hillman Minx, and celebrating this, in September, came the new Series 2 "Jubilee" Minx. A re-designed grille and chromium windscreen surround were the principle identification features, and the overall length was increased slightly by positioning the bumper bars further out from the body. Interior styling was virtually unchanged, but a useful improvement was a foam padded leading edge to the parcel shelf. Separate front seats could now be specified for £15 extra. A mechanical change consisted of a new camshaft which gave a useful increase in torque from 69lbs/ft at 2400rpm to 72lbs/ft at 2200rpm. Maximum bhp was unchanged, but now occurred at 4400rpm, 200 revs lower than before, and these changes resulted in rather more flexible bottom end performance. "Manumatic" two pedal control, by Automotive Products Ltd., consisting of a special clutch with a vacuum servo for disengagement, was now available on the De-Luxe saloon for an extra cost of £56. A rubber windscreen surround, silver painted grille, and the lack of headlamp hoods distinguished the Special saloon externally, whilst inside it featured the steering wheel, floorchange gearlever, instrument panel and separate front seats of the utility Husky model. Plain door trims and a woven cotton headlining were other features of the less expensive Special saloon. Wherever appropriate, the modifications also applied to the recently introduced estate car, with the improved torque engine being perhaps even more beneficial here than in the saloon. With prices now of £748, £794, £898 and £938 for the Special, De-Luxe, Convertible and Estate Car, respectively, the range was continuing to offer good value but was now faced with strong competition from Vauxhall's Victor (£748) and Victor Super (£781) which had appeared earlier in the year.

Meanwhile, the compact utility Husky had continued to be based on the earlier MkIII bodyshell, but was finally brought into line with a new bodyshell, based on the then current Minx series, in January 1958. The new Husky also received the ohv engine, although in a slightly de-tuned state (40bhp at 4000rpm). The Minx saloon gearbox and axle ratios were used, but smaller tyres – 5.00 x 15 – reduced the overall gearing very slightly. At £698, the new Husky was a tempting alternative to the Austin A35 Countryman (£667), or the Ford 100E Squire at £695.

September 1958 saw the introduction of the Series III models, with enlarged capacity engines being the most notable change. An increase in the bore diameter to 79mm resulted in a capacity of 1494cc, and with a compression ratio now of 8.5:1, 49bhp at 4400rpm and 78lbs/ft torque at 2100rpm was available. Lead indium big end bearings – replacing the white metal variety – were

The new 1494 c.c. Hillman Minx Convertible

introduced to cope with the increased loads imposed by the larger capacity, as was a slightly larger diameter clutch.

The opportunity was also taken to raise the overall gearing, with a new axle ratio of 4.55:1 giving 16.1mph:1000rpm in top gear. Criticism had been levelled at the Minx in respect of its indirect ratios of which first gear was extremely low and 2nd and 3rd approximated to the usual 1st and 2nd ratios in a typical three speed box. In an attempt to rectify the situation, the Series III gearbox was equipped with a much higher bottom gear which in fact now brought it very close to the 2nd gear ratio, and in some quarters the box was now criticised for still being in effect, a three-speed gearbox, but with two "bottom" ratios, one of which – 2nd gear actually – was synchronised. Indeed, the rather curious choice of lower ratios was acknowledged in the owners' handbook supplied with the car, with the comment that "It is also advisable to engage first gear occasionally to prevent it from becoming stiff from disuse"!

Overall, the mechanical changes resulted in the Series III model showing a slight improvement in acceleration and speed potential, with noticeably more effortless cruising in the 60/65mph region, and the steady speed fuel consumption, around 35mpg at 50mph, was also good for this class of car. A re-designed, full-width grille easily identified the latest Minx, and the De-Luxe models also now featured a narrow chrome strip running the full length of the car between wheelarch and window level.

Continuing an annual up-dating policy, the Rootes Group announced further modifications to the Minx range in September 1959, with the latest models being designated Series IIIA. A redesigned grille and a new windscreen which was both deeper and wider than before were visible alterations at the front. At the rear, a new upper wing shape gave the effect of fins which were flattened outwards, and beneath these were new vertical oval clusters containing the rear lamps and direction indicator lights. The headlamp hoods of the De-Luxe cars were now painted to match the body colour. Inside, a new front seat featured latex foam cushioning; and the vynide trim was of a new texture.

A new inlet and exhaust manifold, with a larger Zenith carburettor gave a further small increase in the power and torque. The 4.55:1 axle was retained, but the gearbox now had new indirect ratios of which the unsynchronised bottom gear was lowered again, but not as low as in the original installation, and the 2nd and 3rd gear ratios were raised; giving a more even spread. A short floor-mounted lever now controlled the gearbox on the home market cars, with the column change still being a Minx feature for overseas markets. Apart from the Special saloon, the IIIA models were equipped with brake drums of 1 inch larger diameter than before, and Burman recirculating ball steering gear replaced the previous worm and nut arrangement. Purchase tax reductions earlier in the year had reduced prices considerably, and the Series IIIA Special and De-Luxe saloons were now listed at £722 and £764.

For a further £124, the Minx buyer could now specify fully automatic transmission. The system chosen was the Smiths "Easidrive" in which two separate magnetic couplings replaced the fluid torque converter found more usually in automatic transmissions. The gearbox had three forward speeds, and gear changing was by means of a solenoid connected to an electrical

The exhilarating

HILLMAN

Minx de Luxe Saloon
Minx Convertible
Minx Estate Car
Minx Special Saloon

a better buy because it's better built !

ROOTES MOTORS LIMITED

HILLMAN MOTOR CAR CO. LTD · DIVISION OF ROOTES MOTORS LTD · LONDON SHOWROOMS & EXPORT DIVISION · ROOTES LTD · DEVONSHIRE HOUSE · LONDON W.1

Further styling changes for 1960 resulted in the designation Series IIIA. The Smiths 'Easidrive' automatic transmission was introduced as an option on this model.

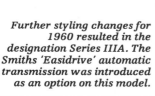

By 1962 the Minx was known simply as Minx 1600, this title referring to the 1594cc engine which the model had received late in 1961.

control unit and a governor driven by a cable from the rear of the gearbox. The accelerator pedal was also linked to the governor, with gear changes thus depending upon both road speed and engine load. A kickdown facility to engage a lower ratio was also provided, and a second gear "hold" position could be selected on the column mounted lever. The electrical control system of the "Easidrive" transmission had its own separate wiring harness.

The Hillman Husky still retained the 1390cc unit, but now acquired the improved manifolding of the Minx IIIA which increased its power output to 47bhp at 4400rpm. In March 1960 it received the improved gearbox ratios and the short gearchange lever, at which time it also acquired the deeper windscreen of the Minx IIIA. Later in 1960, the entire range received an internal gearbox modification which included a re-designed mainshaft, and in October a hypoid bevel final drive unit replaced the spiral bevel drive. This new rear axle unit had a ratio of 4.44:1, thus increasing the overall gearing very slightly. The basic Minx now lost its "Special" title and was upgraded to nearer the De-Luxe model. The grille was the same style as the De-Luxe, but in polished aluminium rather than chrome: the De-Luxe-style instrument panel replaced the spartan Husky-style panel previously used. The Minx range was now designated IIIB, and continued as such until August 1961 when the fitting of a larger capacity engine of 1594cc resulted in the designation IIIC. The new engine was basically a larger bored version of the same unit; and soon after its adoption the designation IIIC disappeared to be replaced by the title Minx 1600.

Development and production of the Minx range continued well into the 1960s, and although there was not a Series IV model a Series V did appear in 1963, and displayed such considerable differences to the outer panelwork and the roof and rear window line that it bore little visual resemblance to the Series I-III from which it had evolved.

Hillman New Minx Series I/II/III

	Series I (Series II)	Series III
Engine	4 cyl, ohv	4 cyl, ohv
Capacity	1390cc	1494cc
Bore	76.2mm	79mm
Stroke	76.2mm	76.2mm
Compression ratio	8.0:1	8.5:1
Max BHP	47.5 @ 4600rpm (47.5 @ 4400rpm)	49 @ 4400rpm
Max torque	69lbs/ft @ 2400rpm (72lbs/ft @ 2200rpm)	78lbs/ft @ 2100rpm
Gearing	15.3mph/1000rpm	16.1mph/1000rpm
Tyres	5.60 x 15	5.60 x 15
Kerb weight	19 1/2cwt	19 1/2cwt

Performance

	"The Autocar" 27th July 1956	"The Autocar" 14th November 1958
Max speed:		
Top gear	77.5mph (mean) 82.7mph (best)	77.6mph (mean) 82.0mph (best)
3rd gear	60mph	58mph
2nd gear	36mph	35mph
1st gear	24mph	28mph
Acceleration:		
0-30mph	6.7 seconds	6.8 seconds
0-50mph	17.6 seconds	17.2 seconds
0-60mph	27.7 seconds	26.6 seconds
0-70mph	46.1 seconds	43.8 seconds
	Top gear/3rd gear	Top gear/3rd gear
20-40mph	12.2/7.9 seconds	11.8/8.0 seconds
30-50mph	15.0/10.6 seconds	13.2/10.2 seconds
40-60mph	17.5/16.8 seconds	16.1/– seconds
Fuel consumption	34.3mpg (287 miles)	28.6mpg (2277 miles)

Chapter 5
Morris

Minor
Series MM/
Series II/
1000 (948cc)

Although not actually announced until Britain staged its first postwar Motor Show at Earls Court in October 1948, development of the Morris Minor Series MM had in fact begun during the darkest days of world war two.

A prototype car – named Mosquito – which, apart from being somewhat narrow bore a remarkable resemblance to the eventual Minor of 1948, first ran in 1943. The Mosquito was almost wholly the brainchild of Alec Issigonis, a gifted engineer who had worked for Morris since before the war, and who was of course to become world-famous many years later as the creator of the remarkable Mini.

The integral body/chassis structure of the Mosquito showed a mild transatlantic influence in its styling features despite its compact size, and clothed an advanced mechanical specification. Independent front suspension in which horizontal fore and aft torsion bars replaced the springs, rack and pinion steering gear, and longitudinally mounted rear leaf springs were all features which would appear on the production model. However, the Mosquito's horizontally opposed, or "flat" four-cylinder sidevalve engine, and the three-speed gearbox with steering column mounted lever did not survive the development programme, and when the Minor appeared it was powered by a conventional in-line engine. This engine was in fact the final version of the ageing sidevalve unit which Morris had derived from the Ford 8hp Y type which had been dismantled by Morris back in 1932.

The engine had in fact already been considerably up-dated, by the adoption of a counterbalanced crankshaft and replaceable shell bearings, for the Morris 8 Series E of 1939, although it was still without a water pump and oil filter in its latest application. With bore and stroke measurements of 57mm x 90mm giving a capacity of 918cc, a compression ratio of 6.6:1 and a single SU carburettor fed by a bulkhead mounted SU electric fuel pump, the engine produced 27.5bhp at 4400rpm and 39lbs/ft torque at 2400rpm. The four-speed gearbox, with synchromesh between the three upper ratios and a floor-mounted gearchange was also substantially that of the Series E, and was transmitting the power to a new rear-axle with a ratio of 4.55:1 which gave quite high overall gearing for this size of car, with 15mph per 1000rpm in top gear. Roadwheels of 14 inch diameter with 5.50 section tyres, and a Lockheed all hydraulic braking system in which the master cylinder was rather curiously placed in a most inaccessible position under the floor, and featuring 7 inch diameter drums all round completed the technical specification.

The two-door bodyshell was amply braced in its lower regions by the sills running along each side of the floorpan, and an inverted U-section stiffener under the rear seat position. Chassis type rails ran forward of the substantial bulkhead structure to act as engine mounts, and slightly to the rear of the bulkhead to meet another transverse member on which were the torsion bar attachment points. The curved, and quite wide bonnet opened from its rear edge and gave good accessibility to most components requiring routine attention, including the battery which was mounted centrally on the bulkhead just above engine height. At the rear, the curved boot featured a wooden floor beneath which was kept the spare wheel and tools. A low mounted 5 gallon fuel tank also resided here, the neck of its long filler tube protruding from the nearside rear lower bodywork. Full advantage was taken of the lack of any bracing behind the rear

Overleaf. Beautifully restored Morris Minor Series MM Convertible. Insets on right show one of the earliest MM saloons still in existence and a later Series MM saloon with headlamps in wings. Insets on left show three pages from the original sales brochure.

Thoroughly tested, new from radiator badge to rear bumper, the *MORRIS MINOR* brings motoring perfection within reach by satisfying your ideals *and* your pocket

The New

MORRIS MINOR

The World's

Supreme Small Car

Supreme in Performance

Supreme in Economy

seat by providing a fold-forward rear seat squab, thus usefully increasing the luggage space if required when the rear seats were unoccupied.

The passenger compartment was neatly trimmed, with the seats and side trim being in the then relatively new Vynide material. A cloth roof-lining and a fully carpeted floor also helped to give a comfortable appearance to the interior. Armrests were provided in the rear side panels, but were omitted from the rather plain door-trims. Both doors did however feature window winding mechanism and swivelling quarter windows. A gold coloured facia with a central panel of vertical chrome bars looked somewhat transatlantic. A circular speedometer, flanked by instruments for fuel level and engine oil pressure faced the driver, these being viewed through a sprung three-spoked steering wheel. The opposite side of the facia panel was in fact the lid of a glove compartment, and featured a circular Morris emblem. A full width parcel shelf of useful depth ran beneath the facia panel. A windscreen wiper was provided on the driver's side only of the split, V screen. External embellishment consisted of a chrome plated finish to the simple mesh grille and its wider surround which also embraced the low-set headlamps. The bumpers, hubcaps, door-handles and window frames, centre screen pillar, boot and bonnet hinges, and badges also featured a chromium

The raised headlamps appeared on the later MM models, and the 1952 car pictured here also differs slightly from the earlier model by the adoption of a painted finish for the grille.

finish, whilst the raised body waistline moulding was highlighted by a painted coachline.

A convertible, the Minor Tourer, accompanied the saloon in production from the start, and boasted similar trim and equipment, including the wind-up windows in the front. Slight strengthening, principally reinforcing of the sills, went some way towards compensating for the lack of a steel roof.

With its price of £358 being only £48 more than the still basically pre-war Ford Anglia, the new Minor was offering outstanding value for money in this class. In terms of straight-line performance, with a maximum speed of just over 60mph and requiring around 35 seconds to reach 50mph from rest, the Minor was no better than its rivals. However, its roadholding and handling qualities were setting completely new standards which would enable it to attain average journey times quite beyond the reach of contemporary rivals.

A four-door Minor joined the range in October 1950, by which time several useful improvements had already been included in the Minor's specification. An interior heater was now available as an extra-cost option, thanks to the fact that a water pump could now also be specified. An engine oil filter was another improvement and came as standard, whilst the bodywork was better protected now by an improved paint process. In order to meet lighting regulations

The bonnet top motif is the only outward indication that this is a Series II car with the ohv engine.

A 1954 advertisement for the Series II Morris Minor.

The straight gearlever of the ohv cars combined with a split windscreen identified this as a Series II. In other respects the interior was little changed from the MM models.

The re-styled facia with central speedometer of the later Series II Morris Minor models made its appearance in October 1954.

there, Minors for the American market had featured headlamps in a raised position, and this arrangement was a further distinguishing feature on the new four-door models for the home market as well, although it was to be a short time yet before the raised headlamps became standard throughout the range. Priced at £569, the four-door model seemed somewhat expensive alongside the two-door saloon and Tourer which were now both being offered at £383. The four-door car did however offer further small additional refinements on top of the convenience of the extra doors, with an interior light, ashtrays, front door straps, and twin windscreen wipers being standard equipment.

In mid-1952 the Series MM was joined in production by the Series II which was at first available for export only, not actually becoming the standard model until early in 1953, when the Series MM was phased out. The principle feature of the Series II was the 803cc engine, and the drive train straight out of the Austin A30, the two former rival companies having by this time merged to form the British Motor Corporation. Complete with an SU carburettor in its new Morris installation, the 803cc ohv unit produced 30bhp at 4800rpm, and a reduction in the overall gearing, now 13.1mph per 1,000rpm, compensated for the fact that the new engine was some 115cc smaller than its predecessor. However, the Minor was a rather heavy car by 800cc standards, and so the small increase in net power output resulted only in a useful, rather than startling increase in acceleration, whilst open-road cruising was somewhat more fussy now on the lower gearing. Fuel consumption, with an overall figure of around 37/38mpg was largely unchanged. Surprisingly, the only external identification feature on the Series II was a new style "M" bonnet motif.

The range was expanded in October 1953 with the addition of an estate car variation – the Minor Traveller. Retaining the saloon's front end structure – including the doors – and the original floorpan, the Traveller featured ash-framed aluminium panelled rear bodywork with steel rear wings similar in style, although not exactly the same as those of the saloon. Large all-round windows – those in

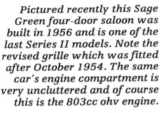

Pictured recently this Sage Green four-door saloon was built in 1956 and is one of the last Series II models. Note the revised grille which was fitted after October 1954. The same car's engine compartment is very uncluttered and of course this is the 803cc ohv engine.

the side being sliding – gave an airy effect to the interior, access to which for loading was excellent via the two rear doors – also wood framed – which opened from the centre. The Traveller was available in both standard (£599) and De-Luxe (£622) versions, and was offering good value for those seeking a compact, yet quite roomy load carrier of obviously sturdy construction. The De-Luxe specification included a heater, passenger sunvisor, leather seat facings, and bumper overriders, and it was not long afterwards that saloons and Tourers equipped to this level became available for a similar £23 increase over the cost of the basic models, which by now were themselves listed at £529 and £560 in two or four-door form.

Slightly re-styled seating was phased in during 1954, and in October that year an external styling change consisted of a new simple grille of horizontal painted slats (the original mesh grille had in fact also lost its plated finish some time earlier) with a thin chromium surround. A completely re-styled facia appeared at the same time, with the circular speedometer now centrally placed and flanked by a cubby hole on each side. The fuel level gauge was incorporated in the speedometer, with the oil pressure gauge now giving way to a warning light.

In September 1956, the Minor was at last made available with a power unit which would provide a level of performance much more in keeping with the car's excellent all-round road manners. This engine was of course the 948cc development of the BMC A-series unit, complete with an improved gearbox and a higher rear axle ratio (see Austin A35). In addition to the new "Minor 1000" badges, there were other recognition features amongst which was one very notable improvement: a deeper and wider one piece curved windscreen. It was something of a surprise however, that this new screen was still accompanied by the original wipers which left a large unwiped area in the centre. A larger rear window was also new, as were rear wings with a smaller wheel arch cut-out that more closely matched the diameter of the tyre. Inside, the layout remained substantially as before, but the two facia cubby holes now acquired lids; whilst a new dished steering wheel, still of sprung three spoked design, faced the driver. Sprouting from the steering column was as early example of

Rearward view was much improved on the Minor 1000. The separate flashing indicators situated above the rear lamp units are a non-original addition to this preserved example.

Identifying the Minor 1000 was the one-piece windscreen and considerably increased glass area. The slatted grille had first appeared on the later Series II.

the multi-purpose stalk, operating in this case the horn and the direction indicators which, surprisingly, were still of the semaphore type. As had been the case with the previous engine, the Morris installation again included an SU carburettor; this feature raising the power output from the Austin's 34bhp to 37bhp in the Minor. The performance inprovement over the Series II was quite considerable, with an ability to exceed 70mph being accompanied by acceleration from rest to 50 and 60mph in around 18 and 30 seconds. Overall fuel consumption was still in the 35/40mpg bracket, and figures in excess of 45mpg could be obtained with steady main-road cruising in the 45/50mph range.

Although now eight years old, the Minor had been given a considerable new lease of life, and sales increased throughout 1957. During that year, a $6\frac{1}{2}$ gallon fuel tank was introduced, but apart from this the model continued virtually unchanged until late in 1958, at which time softer rear springs – 5 leaves instead of the original 7 – were adopted in the interest of improved riding comfort.

The millionth Morris Minor left the production line in December 1960; it and the following 349 cars receiving a special lilac paint scheme, white leather upholstery and "Minor 1000000" badges. Despite more modern rivals from elsewhere and its own BMC stable, the Minor was destined to continue in production throughout the 1960s, so becoming in its later years a "timeless" model which would continue to satisfy the demands of many who had no desire to be forever keeping up with changing motoring fashions.

Datapanel: Morris Minor Series MM/Series II/1000 (948cc)

	Series MM	Series II/(1000)
Engine	4 cyl, sidevalve	4 cyl, ohv
Capacity	918cc	803cc (948cc)
Bore	57mm	58mm (63 mm)
Stroke	90mm	76.2mm
Compression ratio	6.6:1	7.2:1 (8.3:1)
Max BHP	27.5 @ 4400rpm	30 @ 4800rpm (37 @ 4750rpm)
Max torque	37lbs/ft @ 2400rpm	40 @ 2400rpm (50 @ 2500rpm)
Gearing	15mph/1000rpm	13.1mph/1000rpm (15.2/1000rpm)
Tyres	5.00 x 14	5.00 x 14
Kerb weight	15 1/2cwt (16 cwt 4 door)	15cwt (15 1/2 cwt 4 door)
Overall length	12ft 4in	12ft 4in
Overall width	5ft 1in	5ft 1in
Wheelbase	7ft 2in	7ft 2in

Performance

	"The Autocar" Road Tests 1951 MM 4 door	"The Autocar" Road Tests 1961 1000 (948cc)
Max speed:		
Top gear	61mph (mean) —	73.1mph (mean) 76.0mph (best)
3rd gear	46mph	60mph
2nd gear	31mph	34mph
1st gear	19mph	22mph
Acceleration:		
0-30mph	9.8 seconds	7.2 seconds
0-50mph	38.5 seconds	18.8 seconds
0-60mph	—	32.6 seconds
	Top gear/3rd gear	Top gear/3rd gear
20-40mph	23.4/14.2 seconds	14.6/9.9 seconds
30-50mph	36.8/– seconds	17.9/12.6 seconds
40-60mph	–/– seconds	26.1/23.9 seconds
Fuel consumption	35/40mpg	34.7mpg (1177 miles)

Chapter 5
Morris

Oxford
Series MO/
Six
Series MS

Announced at the same time as the Minor, October 1948, completing the updated Morris range came the Series MO Oxford and Series MS Six saloons. Considerably larger than the Minor, but otherwise very similarly styled, the Oxford and Six were 1 1/2 and 2 1/4-litre saloons which shared an identical bodyshell from the windscreen rearwards. At the front, the two cars differed according to the length of the engine, with the four-cylinder Oxford having a relatively short engine compartment with a curved bonnet top similar to that of the Minor; and a wide low set chrome plated grille. The engine compartment of the six-cylinder car was considerably longer, resulting in a wheelbase which, at 9ft 2in, was over 1ft longer than on the Oxford. The bonnet top of the Six continued horizontally to the front where a traditionally styled upright radiator grille was effectively styled into the modern flowing lines. The combined head and sidelamp units were incorporated into the smoothly styled wings in both cases.

All four doors were hinged at the front; and all were equipped with separate quarter windows – swivelling in the front – and winding mechanism to lower the main windows. Strap type doorpulls were featured in the front, whilst the rear doors were fitted with combined armrest/doorpulls. Bench seats were provided, that in the

A 1949 advertisement depicting an early MO Oxford, and showing something of the worldwide esteem in which British cars were then held.

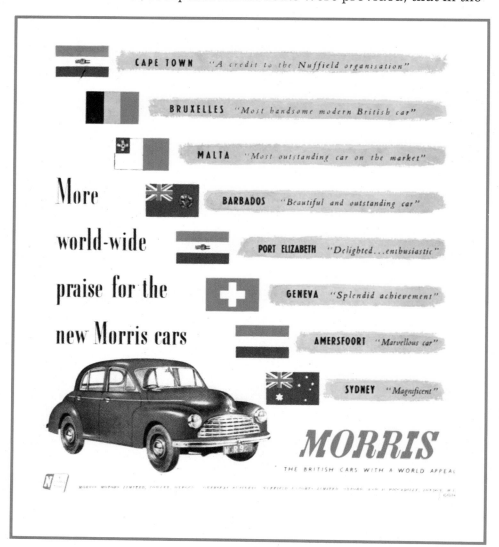

CAPE TOWN *"A credit to the Nuffield organisation"*

BRUXELLES *"Most handsome modern British car"*

MALTA *"Most outstanding car on the market"*

BARBADOS *"Beautiful and outstanding car"*

PORT ELIZABETH *"Delighted...enthusiastic"*

GENEVA *"Splendid achievement"*

AMERSFOORT *"Marvellous car"*

SYDNEY *"Magnificent"*

More world-wide praise for the new Morris cars

MORRIS

THE BRITISH CARS WITH A WORLD APPEAL

front compartment being upholstered in leather. The rear seat – upholstered in vinyl – was usefully wider; making these cars comfortable five-seaters when necessary, and was equipped with a pull-down central armrest. The facia included a well-equipped instrument panel in the centre, consisting of a large circular speedometer, matching electric clock, and ammeter and gauges for engine oil pressure and fuel tank contents. A plain panel faced the driver, with a matching glovebox lid ahead of the passenger. A deep, full width parcel shelf ran beneath the facia. Standard equipment included twin windscreen wipers, a single sunvisor and a single horn – this being operated by a button in the centre of the sprung three-spoked steering wheel.

The curved boot lid was held open with a self supporting stay, and in this position revealed a reasonably roomy luggage compartment whilst also giving access to the horizontally mounted spare wheel beneath. The boot was illuminated automatically when the lid was open. A chrome finish was applied to the bumpers, hubcaps, door handles, boot and bonnet hinges in addition to the radiator grilles, whilst the door window frames were in stainless steel.

Opening the rear hinged bonnet on the Oxford revealed a four-cylinder sidevalve engine of 1476cc, a capacity arrived at with a bore and stroke of 73.5mm and 87mm, respectively. A single SU carburettor was supplied from the 9 gallon tank by a bulkhead mounted SU electric fuel pump. The tank was situated under the nearside rear of the car. With a compression ratio of 6.8:1 the engine produced 40.5bhp at 4200rpm. Of identical bore and stroke, the six-cylinder unit had a capacity of 2215cc. A single SU again supplied the mixture, but in other respects the engine differed markedly from that in the Oxford, being of the overhead valve type. Carried in-line in the cylinder head, the valves were operated by a single overhead camshaft driven by a skew gear at the top of a vertical shaft, which itself was driven by skew gears from the crankshaft. Hardened steel mushroom tappets were threaded into the valve stems with the clearance being held by a lock-nut. Extremely accurate clearances were possible with this method, but, partly due to the fact that the valves did not rotate in use, this engine tended to suffer rather badly in service from burned-out valves. With a compression ratio of 7.0:1 the unit developed 70bhp at 4800rpm.

A conventional four-speed gearbox, with the ratios selected by a column-mounted lever, and with a rather low unsynchronised bottom gear transmitted the power via an open propeller shaft to a hypoid rear axle. The axle ratios were 4.55:1 and 4.1:1, respectively, for the four- and six-cylinder models giving overall gearing of 16.0mph per 1000rpm and 18.8mph per 1000rpm.

Independent front suspension of the torsion bar and wishbone type was a feature of both models, as were half-elliptic leaf springs at the rear. The direction of the front wheels was controlled by rack and pinion steering gear on the Oxford; whereas on the Six the longer nose necessitated a different layout, and a Bishop Cam Gear arrangement was adopted. The Lockheed all hydraulic braking system featured 8 inch diameter drums on the Oxford, with 89 square inches of lining area, and 10 inch drums on the higher powered car, these having shoes with 134 square inches of lining.

With prices of £546 and £671 these new Morris models were

Flashing direction indicators have been added to this restored Oxford which was recently posed before the camera to show off the rear-end styling to good effect.

The wooden-framed bodywork of the Oxford Traveller gave something of the traditional "Shooting Brake" look.

A longer nose and rather more traditionally styled radiator grille characterized the six-cylinder model. RKE 803 is a preserved example built in 1953.

Get to know this magnificent Morris Oxford. Experience the delight of its smooth-riding and controllability, made possible by torsion-bar suspension. Sense the feeling of spirited power when the highway invites speed. Then examine it for finish and styling. You'll discover it has "Quality First" in all its features. Ownership will prove that traditional Morris reliability is an investment in long-lasting value.

All seats within wheelbase: *All seating within the wheelbase (where seats should be for comfort) provide lounge-easy riding throughout the longest journey.*

Phenomenal luggage space: *10 cubic feet of luggage space is devoted to luggage exclusively, enough room for the items needed for long-vacation touring. The spare wheel is in a separate compartment.*

Superfine finishes: *Seven coats of paint go on to a dipped rust-proof surface. The brilliant colours keep their showroom freshness over years of hard service.*

You'll be glad you bought a

"QUALITY FIRST"

MORRIS Oxford

MORRIS MINOR • MORRIS OXFORD • MORRIS SIX

Morris Motors Ltd., Cowley, Oxford. Overseas Business: Nuffield Exports Ltd., Oxford, and 41 Piccadilly, London, W.1

C.134D(53)

offering sound value in their class with a relatively high standard of trim and finish for these prices. On the road, with only 40bhp to cope with an unladen weight of 21cwt the Oxford required some 46/47 seconds to reach 60mph from rest, but would continue to a maximum just short of 70mph. Fuel consumption would usually be in the 28 to 32mpg range. The six-cylinder car did of course provide a much livelier performance, in spite of an increase in weight of 4cwt, with a maximum speed of rather more than 80mph and acceleration from rest to 70mph in around 36 seconds. Both cars quickly gained a good reputation in respect of general roadworthiness.

Improvements phased in during 1949 included, in the Oxford, a revised cooling system which was now pressurised, a reduction in the indirect gear ratios – thus sharpening up the acceleration slightly – and telescopic dampers in place of the original lever-arm type at the rear. Angled inwards, these dampers eliminated the Panhard-type anti-sway bar which had been an original Oxford feature. 5.50 section tyres now replaced the earlier 5.25 section variety, and the bulkhead mounted fuel pump changed sides in order to be further away from the heat of the exhaust manifold. Other changes which applied to both cars were improved windscreen sealing, twin sunvisors, twin windtone horns, and a rexine rooflining in place of the previous cloth. Visible changes included twin rear lamps and a high mounted square number plate in place of the earlier low set oblong type.

The policy of continued development was maintained throughout much of 1950, during which time both cars were given lower axle ratios in order to improve acceleration. On the Oxford, a change in the combustion chamber shape adjacent to the valves actually lowered the compression ratio slightly – to 6.6:1 – but improved the gas flow to such an extent that the bhp was increased from 40.5 at 4200rpm to 41 at 4000rpm. A larger radiator was another new Oxford feature, whilst on the Six the damping was improved by the introduction of twin dampers in each of the independent front suspension units. A visible change was the adoption of separate sidelights at the front, positioned in the wings just beneath the headlamps. The acceleration of both cars had been usefully improved, although at the expense of a distinctly lower maximum speed in the case of the Six, and as the prices remained unchanged, the range was continuing to offer good value in what was becoming a hotly contested market sector.

An addition to the range came in September 1952, with the announcement of the Oxford Traveller. Identical in appearance to the saloon forward of the centre pillar, the Traveller was in fact built on a separate chassis frame. Aluminium panelling of the ash-framed estate car rear bodywork was used to offset the weight increase imposed by the separate chassis, nevertheless, the unladen weight still went up to 22cwt in this configuration. A re-designed grille appeared on the Oxford models later in 1952, of similar outline to the original but now with three wide horizontal bars and in stainless steel rather than chrome plate. The Six was now improved with a re-designed cylinder head in which the water jacketing arrangements gave much better valve stem cooling and so eliminated the problem of valve stem distortion which sometimes afflicted this engine. The new head gave a reduction in the compression ratio to 6.6:1 and although the quoted power output remained the same at 70bhp, it now came lower down the revolution range at 4400rpm.

Prices for saloons were now £794 and £997, with the Oxford Traveller coming at £825. Price reductions during 1953 kept the range competitive, and at Earls Court that year the saloons were divided into standard and De-Luxe categories with the standard models being offered at £703 and £844 for the Oxford and Six, respectively. The extra cost De-Luxe specification included leather upholstery, heater, and bumper over-riders. The range now continued until May 1954 when replaced by the new Series II models.

Datapanel: Morris Oxford Series MO/Six Series MS

	Oxford	Six
Engine	*4 cyl, sidevalve*	*6 cyl, sohc*
Capacity	*1476cc*	*2215cc*
Bore	*73.5mm*	*73.5mm*
Stroke	*87mm*	*87mm*
Compression ratio	*6.8:1 (6.6:1 later)*	*7.0:1 (6.6:1 later)*
Max BHP	*40.5 @ 4200rpm*	*70 @ 4800rpm*
	(41 @ 4000rpm later)	*(70 @ 4400rpm later)*
Gearing	*16mph/1000rpm (4.55 axle)*	*18.8mph/1000rpm (4.1 axle)*
	15mph/1000rpm (4.875 axle)	*17mph/1000rpm (4.55 axle)*
Tyres	*5.50 x 15*	*6.00 x 15*
Kerb weight	*21cwt*	*25cwt*
Overall length	*13ft 11in*	*14ft 9in*
Overall width	*5ft 5in*	*5ft 5in*
Wheelbase	*8ft 1in*	*9ft 2in*

Performance

	Oxford	Six
	"The Autocar Road Tests 1951" 4.55/1 axle	*"The Motor" RT No.12/50 4.1/1 axle*
Max speed:		
Top gear	*67mph (mean)*	*82.5mph (mean)*
	–	*85.5mph (best)*
3rd gear	*47mph*	*62mph*
2nd gear	*32mph*	*42mph*
1st gear	*19mph*	*not recorded*
Acceleration:		
0-30mph	*9.7 seconds*	*6.4 seconds*
0-50mph	*27.4 seconds*	*15.3 seconds*
0-60mph	*46.7 seconds*	*22.4 seconds*
0-70mph	*–*	*36.6 seconds*
	Top gear/3rd gear	*Top gear/3rd gear*
20-40mph	*15.4/11.4 seconds*	*12.0/8.0 seconds*
30-50mph	*19.3/– seconds*	*12.5/8.9 seconds*
40-60mph	*–/– seconds*	*14.2/– seconds*
50-70mph	*–/– seconds*	*20.2/– seconds*
Fuel consumption	*27-30mpg*	*20.0mpg (185 miles)*

Chapter 5
Morris

Oxford
Series
II/III/
Cowley/
Isis

Announced in May 1954, the Series II Morris Oxford was a considerable advance in many respects over the likeable sidevalve-engined MO Series which had re-established the Oxford name in the early postwar years. As a direct result of the merger between Austin and Morris in 1952, the new Oxford was inevitably something of a hybrid, however, the marriage of Austin and Morris features proved to be a particularly happy one in this case.

The full-width four door bodyshell was of monocoque construction, braced underneath at the front by a pair of longitudinal U-section members which terminated where they met a transverse

Today's good news!

THE

ALL NEW

"QUALITY FIRST" MORRIS

OXFORD

(SERIES II)

IS HERE !

Here's news for every motorist — a great new Morris Oxford! Here is a *family car* that offers something fresh in value-for-money, *family car performance*.
The new 1½ litre O.H.V. engine will astonish and delight you with its power and flexibility. It is fast, lively and economical, capable of sustained high cruising speed and impressive acceleration-off-the-mark.
It is easy to drive, beautifully styled in the modern manner, with a wonderfully spacious, comfortable and well appointed interior.
Meet it soon... *The sooner the better!*

more **Power...**
more **Room...**
more **Comfort**

SAFETY GLASS ALL ROUND

SERVICE IN EUROPE
Qualified Morris owners planning a Continental Tour are invited to see their Morris dealer for details of a free service to save foreign currency.

MORRIS MOTORS LIMITED, COWLEY, OXFORD.
London Distributors: Morris House, Berkeley Square, W.1.
Overseas Business: Nuffield Exports Ltd., Oxford, & 41 Piccadilly, London, W.1.

An advertisement from May 1954, announcing the new Series II Oxford and still featuring the Morris "Quality First" theme.

The flashing indicators beneath the headlamps and repeaters in the front wings are recent and non-original additions to this well-preserved example of the Cowley model.

That proves it —

I'M GOING TO

HAVE A MORRIS

"QUALITY FIRST"

MORRIS
Oxford

Ease of entry and exit and a roomy interior were excellent Oxford features.

stiffener under the front seat position. Similar U-section members ran from a position under the rear seat to the rear end of the car. Chrome plated bumpers – complete with over-riders – and with their mounting points attached to the extremes of the U-section members offered front and rear protection. The chromium radiator grille followed closely the design of that of the previous model, and so easily distinguished this newcomer from BMC as a Morris. Chrome plating was also applied to the external bonnet and boot lid hinges, headlamp surrounds, door handles, window frames, hub caps and a front wing rubbing strip.

Wide, front hinged doors allowed particularly easy access to a passenger compartment in which full-width bench seats entirely justified the six-seater claim. The equipment and furnishings were very definitely to De-Luxe standards. Swivelling front quarter windows, window winding mechanism in all four doors, a washable vinyl roof lining, twin sun visors, leather upholstery, fitted carpets and a heater unit were all included in the standard specification. The rear doors were provided with doorpull/armrests, whilst strap-type door-pulls were featured in the front compartment. A full circle horn ring adorned the two-spoke steering wheel which was mounted on a column which itself was unusual in that it was offset slightly to the offside; this arrangement being chosen to allow the driver to "sit in the corner" so to speak when the front seat was fully occupied.

Comprehensive instrumentation was housed in twin dials mounted centrally in the facia, one for the speedometer, milometer and trip recorder, the other featuring gauges for oil pressure, water temperature, fuel level, and an ammeter. The instrument panel was flanked on each side by usefully deep parcel shelves. Beneath the panel was a neat row of identical switches for the wipers, choke, starter etc., which were however completely out of the reach of anyone sitting in a normal driving position: their operation necessitating a considerable lean forward, across and downwards by the driver. The electric windscreen wipers were self-parking but in spite of the large single piece screen, were curiously arranged as on cars with a split screen and so left a large unwiped area in the centre. Semaphore indicators were another surprise on a completely new model at a time when flashing indicators were being adopted elsewhere.

At the front, the rear-hinged bonnet had to be propped open with a stay; whilst at the rear, although not counterbalanced, the wide boot lid did have the benefit of a self-locking strut. With the 12 gallon fuel tank being mounted transversely behind the rear seat the Oxford provided a roomy and usefully-shaped luggage locker, access to which was made easy due to the rear opening coming right down to bumper level. The spare wheel was conveniently situated in an upright position in the offside, and at night the compartment was illuminated through apertures in the backs of the twin tail lights.

It was under the bonnet where the principal Austin influence was to be found, with power being provided by an enlarged version of the well proven 1200cc ohv. Austin A40 unit. By this time known as the BMC B-series, this latest example was of 1489cc, a capacity arrived at by increasing the bore diameter from 65mm to 73mm whilst leaving the stroke unchanged at 89mm. At this capacity the ample cylinder block still allowed water to circulate completely around each cylinder, and with the crankshaft being counterbalanced and supported in three main bearings of 2 inches in diameter, bottom end rigidity was entirely adequate. Pistons with concave crowns gave a compression ratio of 7.4:1, and with its single SU carburettor – complete with oil bath air-cleaner – and supplied by an SU electric fuel pump situated adjacent to the petrol tank in the boot, the engine developed 50bhp at 4200rpm and 78lbs/ft at 2400rpm. The hydraulically activated clutch was of 8 inches diameter, and a four-speed gearbox was provided, although with rather low indirect ratios of which the unsynchronised bottom gear was so low as to be almost superfluous. Gear selection was by a column-mounted lever which, with a marked lack of precision, fell far short of the standards being set elsewhere for this type of change. Taken overall, the gearbox was the least satisfactory aspect of the Oxford's mechanical specification. An open propeller shaft and a hypoid final drive assembly, with a ratio of 4.875:1 giving overall gearing of 15mph per 1000rpm, completed the transmission.

Excellent road manners had been a feature of the previous Oxford, and in this respect the Series II would carry on the tradition. Rack and pinion steering gear – in which the rack was mounted behind the engine – was chosen once again, as was a wishbone and torsion bar independent front suspension system. The vertical telescopic hydraulic shock absorbers featured cooling fins around their lower circumference, an arrangement chosen to keep the fluid temperature at a low level during fast driving over poor road surfaces. Similar units at the rear controlled the action of the leaf springs on which were carried the live rear axle. The Lockheed hydraulic braking system consisted of 9 inch diameter drums on all four wheels, housing shoes with a total lining area of 99 square inches, an adequate although by no means impressive figure for a $21\frac{3}{4}$cwt car. The brake pedal, like that of the clutch, came up through the floor in the traditional manner. The 15 inch roadwheels were shod with tyres of 5.60 section.

Priced at £744, the Oxford was undercut by its two most obvious rivals; the Vauxhall Wyvern (£702) and the Ford Consul (£666). However, the Oxford was appreciably better equipped than either of these, and with a maximum speed in the region of 75mph coupled with an ability to reach 60mph from rest in around 28 seconds was offering a broadly similar performance potential. An overall fuel consumption of 28/30mpg was within easy reach, and the new model was greeted with enthusiasm by admirers of the previous Oxford.

Within a matter of weeks, the Oxford was joined by a considerably de-trimmed and lower powered variation which re-introduced the name Cowley to the British motoring scene after an absence of many years. Pvc seating – devoid of central armrests, a plastic coated fabric floorcovering, plain door trims, one sunvisor and a steering wheel with a central horn button were all cost cutting interior features. Externally, chromium was absent from the vertical grille bars and the window surrounds, whilst the bumpers were now without over-riders. Under the bonnet was the basic B-series unit of 1200cc which, with its single SU carburettor produced 42bhp at 4500rpm and 58lbs/ft torque at 2400rpm, both rather meagre figures with which to cope with an unladen weight of 21cwt. A rear axle ratio of 5.125:1 lowered the overall gearing to 14.3mph/1000rpm. Further cost cutting was evident with the adoption of 8 inch diameter brake drums and shoes with a modest 88 square inches lining area. Priced at £702, the Cowley was not nearly so attractive a package as was the Oxford, and although it offered small savings in fuel consumption at modest speeds, above about 40mph the Oxford became progressively the more economical of the two.

At the Earls Court Show in October 1954 the Oxford and Cowley saloons were joined by the Oxford Traveller. The front half of this estate car variation was identical to the Oxford saloon, whereas the rear half was totally new. Clever application of timber strips gave the impression that the rear half was constructed in the traditional "shooting brake" manner. In fact, it was almost wholly of steel construction, with the only pieces of timber which were not just simply decorative being the horizontal beams on each side which supported the roof. Access to the loading area was via double doors at the rear, and as the rear end structure was without side doors the Traveller was a two door model from the passenger's point of view. Stiffer rear springs were employed in order to cope with the extra load potential, otherwise the mechanical specification remained unchanged. At a tax paid total of £822 the Traveller was competitively priced, filling the gap which existed between such as the smaller Hillman Minx and Austin A40 estates at £732 and £766, and the slightly larger Vanguard at £844.

In July 1955 the range was expanded with the addition of the six cylinder Isis. Available as both a saloon and Traveller, the Isis was virtually identical with the Oxford from the windscreen rearwards, whilst under a lengthened front end structure which, unfortunately, gave the car a rather ungainly appearance when viewed from certain angles, was housed the 2.6-litre BMC C-series power unit. This engine had already appeared in the Austin Westminster, and the only change in the Morris application was the adoption of an SU rather than Zenith carburettor. In addition to the increase in length, considerable strengthening was necessary to accommodate the heavier engine, this being achieved by the introduction of diagonal tie bars from the inner wing to the scuttle – these bars being bolted to their attachment points, an additional front crossmember and a strengthened toe board. Uprated front suspension, otherwise similar to the four-cylinder cars was fitted, but the new engine installation necessitated completely different steering arrangements, and Bishop cam steering gear with the steering box and three piece track rod ahead of the front axle line was adopted. A rear axle ratio of 4.1:1 in conjunction with larger tyres – 6.00 x 15 – gave overall gearing of 19.1mph per 1000rpm, whilst 10 inch diameter brake drums allowed an appropriate increase in the brake lining area to 140 square inches with which to cope with the extra speed potential. Both basic and De-Luxe models were available at £801 and £844, prices which put the Isis into direct competition with the well established Ford Zephyr/Zodiac at £754 and £851 and the Vauxhall Velox/Cresta models at £759 and £844. With an ultimate maximum speed of rather more than 85mph and an ability to reach 60mph from rest in around 18 seconds, the Isis had a marginally superior straight line performance than the Ford and Vauxhall rivals, although in the more important matter of top gear acceleration and overtaking ability it was inferior to the lower geared and appreciably more flexible Dagenham and Luton cars.

In October 1956, facelifted versions of the range, with the new

A July 1955 advertisement announcing the new six-cylinder Isis. "Lightning acceleration" is perhaps something of an overstatement!

MEET THE **NEW**

High Performance

SIX CYLINDER

MORRIS ISIS

A spacious luxury car with **astonishing performance**

Here are the highlights of this great new Morris: New 2.6 litre B.M.C. overhead-valve 6-cylinder engine. Lightning acceleration with a top speed that goes with it. A full six-seater with room to spare. Loads of room for luggage in spacious rear compartment. Roadability, cornering and steering all that you could desire. Running costs (in relation to performance) surprisingly low.

The greatest "Quality First" Morris in Morris History

designations Cowley 1500, Oxford Series III, and Isis Series II were revealed at the Earls Court Show. Panelwork changes consisted of a new bonnet top with scooped out flutes on each side, and re-designed rear wings which now gave a mildly finned effect. The Oxford now featured hooded headlamp rims, but these were not included on either the Cowley or Isis, although the latter car now sported a mesh backing to the grille (actually introduced a few weeks earlier), which easily distinguished it from the Oxford when viewed head-on. Improved interiors included gloveboxes on each side of a re-styled instrument panel, and re-positioned switchgear which could now be more easily reached by the driver. A full-width padded facia top and a deeply-dished safety steering wheel were also introduced. Although still the basic model, the Cowley acquired the Oxford's 1489cc engine which, in both models, was uprated slightly by an increase in compression ratio to 8.3:1 which would allow full use to be made of the increased performance/economy potential of premium grade petrols. A re-designed steering column gearchange gave rather more accurate gear selection than previously, and so largely overcame the criticism levelled at the earlier models in this respect. Manumatic two pedal control was to be available at extra cost on the Oxford saloon model only.

The six-cylinder engine in the Isis was also uprated, an increase in the compression ratio raised the power output from 86bhp to 90bhp. The offending column gearchange mechanism was also replaced on this model which now featured a floor-mounted arrangement which was unusual in that the lever was positioned to the right of the driver's seat. Borg Warner overdrive had been available on the Isis since its introduction, and that company's fully automatic gearbox was now to be a further alternative option.

By this time priced at £799 and £848, the Cowley and Oxford were continuing to offer sound value, with the cheaper model now being much more attractive in 1½-litre form. The Isis however, now listed at £911 or £960 with the De-Luxe specification, had so far failed almost completely to make any impact in the inexpensive six-cylinder category, and the recent revisions to its specifications seemed unlikely to alter the situation.

Early in 1957 attractive two tone paint schemes were introduced on the Oxford and Isis models, with the colour division being highlighted by a new chromium plated moulding, and in September that year the rather angular Traveller bodywork gave way to a completely re-styled estate car rear end. The estate car was now based more closely on the saloon body, utilising the four doors –

A recent photograph of an original low mileage example of the early Isis.

Move up

to luxury motoring for under £1,000

Very Personally Yours

WITH CHOICE OF

● **COLOURS:**
Seven single-tone or six duo-tone combinations.

● **UPHOLSTERY:**
Luxury two-colour interior trims in hard-wearing nylon and first quality English leather.

● **MECHANICAL OPTIONS:**
Overdrive and automatic gearbox optional extras.

Backed by B.M.C. affording the most comprehensive service facilities in Europe.

"Quality First"

MORRIS ★ ISIS

The best 6-cylinder value in Britain

Price : De-luxe saloon £640 (plus £321.7.0 p.t.)   Automatic gearbox (opt. extra) £105 plus £52.10.0 p.t.
12 MONTHS' WARRANTY

The two-tone colour combination and revised grille of the later Isis show up well in this 1957 advertisement.

those for the rear passengers featuring slightly altered, squared up window frames — and the saloon rear wings. The new Traveller was without timber decoration and would now only be available as an Oxford derivative, to be known as the Traveller Series IV, with the saloon continuing as the Series III. Soon after this the Isis saloon was phased out, but the popular Cowley and Oxford continued unchanged, remaining in production until early in 1959 when they in turn were replaced by the completely re-styled Farina range.

123

'QUALITY FIRST' MORRIS OXFORD

THE MOST SATISFYING MOMENT IN YOUR MOTORING CAREER . . .

You studied all the brochures. You talked to the salesmen. You discussed it with your family, with your motoring acquaintances, and you followed the reports in the motoring magazines. Gradually the weight of evidence built up. Finally, the decision was made. No one will begrudge you this moment of satisfaction as you contemplate the Morris Oxford you have just driven home. And future reappraisals will time and again vindicate your choice of the car which offers so perfect and so unique a combination of spaciousness, top-gear performance, acceleration, economy, braking response, steering control, and road stability. There is no pride quite so legitimate as that felt by the man who has made a rational and objective choice of a Morris Oxford.

The scooped-out bonnet sides of the Series III Oxford features prominently in this reproduction of a page from an original brochure.

A NOTE OF CHALLENGE IN ITS LINES . . .

Another contemporary brochure reproduction, this time showing the neat two-tone paint scheme of the Series III models to good effect, but "aerodynamic profile" ...?

Recent years have seen many conflicting trends in car design. The new shape of the Morris Oxford is a deliberate synthesis of all that is most desirable in contemporary and traditional thinking.

The Oxford is spacious; and its lines give just a sufficient hint of the comfort within. The Oxford is fast; and its aerodynamic profile permits

no doubt about its ability to deal with traffic under all conditions.

Because its design is *inherently* good, the Oxford is a car which needs no decorative additions to give it visual interest. It has the proud good looks of a thoroughbred—a beauty which derives from strength and therefore can never become dated.

The all-steel Oxford Traveller continued in production – as the Series IV – for some time after the Series III saloons had been phased out. This contemporary advertisement emphasises the model's practicality.

Few of us—men or women—are immune to the fascination of the 'station wagon' or 'shooting brake'. The Morris Oxford Traveller is the latest and most exciting development of this concept and offers the great advantage of an all-steel body.

Armchair comfort for six is yours if required, but when extra loads must be carried the rear seat folds completely flat, putting no less than 50 cubic feet of space instantly at your disposal! Four wide-opening side doors and an upward-opening rear door make the Oxford Traveller triumphantly practical as well as supremely sophisticated. With the elegance and styling of a 'Quality First' saloon car it is suitable for all occasions.

Datapanel: Morris Cowley/Oxford/Isis

	Oxford (Cowley 1200)	Isis
Engine	4 cyl, ohv	6 cyl, ohv
Capacity	1489cc (1200cc)	2639cc
Bore	73mm (65.4mm)	79.3mm
Stroke	89mm	89mm
Compression ratio	7.4:1 (7.2:1)	7.25:1
Max BHP	50 @ 4200rpm (42 @ 4500rpm)	86 @ 4250rpm
Max torque	78lbs/ft @ 2400rpm (58 @ 2400rpm)	124lbs/ft @ 2000rpm
Gearing	15mph/1000rpm (14.3mph/1000rpm)	19.1mph/1000rpm
Tyres	5.50 x 15	6.00 x 15
Kerb weight	22.75cwt (21cwt)	27cwt
Overall length	14ft 2in (14 ft 1in)	14ft 10in
Overall width	5ft 5in	5ft 5in
Wheelbase	8ft 1in	8ft 11in

Performance

	"The Motor" RT No. 29/54 (RT No. 5/55)	"The Autocar" 27th April 1956
Max speed:		
Top gear	74.2mph (mean) (71.9mph) 79.7mph (best) (73.2mph)	85mph (mean) 88mph (best)
3rd gear	58mph (53mph)	68mph
2nd gear	37mph (33mph)	47mph
1st gear	not recorded	29mph
Acceleration:		
0-30mph	6.9 seconds (7.5)	5.5 seconds
0-50mph	18.5 seconds (19.8)	12.8 seconds
0-60mph	28.9 seconds (31.5)	17.8 seconds
0-70mph	–	26.1 seconds
	Top gear/3rd gear	Top gear/3rd gear
20-40mph	12.4 (13.2)/8.6 (8.7) seconds	10.1/7.2 seconds
30-50mph	14.0 (15.7)/12.1 (11.9) seconds	11.2/8.0 seconds
40-60mph	18.4 (19.6)/– seconds	13.7/9.6 seconds
50-70mph	–/–	–/– seconds
Fuel consumption	28.2mpg (1129 miles) (28.0mpg 897 miles)	23mpg (986 miles)

Performance figures in brackets are for the Cowley 1200

**Chapter 6
Standard**

**Vanguard
Phase I/II**

Announced in July 1947, the completely new Standard Vanguard was the result of a two year development programme in which the demands of world wide markets had been given much consideration. The Vanguard was intended to replace the entire range of existing Standard products (basically their pre-war range) by the middle of the following year, at which time the company would settle down to a "one model policy" for the forseeable future.

The backbone of the Vanguard was a box-section chassis with a deep cruciform bracing of the centre section, with two outriggers on each side – both within the wheelbase – forming sturdy jacking points. Apart from the relatively narrow transverse member at the extreme rear there was no chassis bracing aft of the rear axle line, and in fact, the rear end of the car as a whole relied on the bodywork for adequate torsional rigidity.

Of six light, four door design, the full-width bodywork was of all steel construction. Its styling – which gave it something of the look of a scaled down Hudson Commodore – displaying a rather surprising degree of transatlantic influence for a product of a wholly British company. Protection at each end was by substantial chrome plated bumpers; their attachment points being the ends of the full length chassis members. The counterbalanced bonnet was hinged at the rear, although due to its narrowing almost to a point at the front, underbonnet accessibility was still somewhat restricted due to the high full-width front wings. A low set grille of chromed horizontal bars, and chrome plated surrounds for the faired-in combined headlamp/sidelamp units completed the rather discreet frontal embellishment.

The steeply curved back end gave a compact overall length of 13 feet 8 inches, which, nevertheless concealed a quite roomy luggage boot. Access to this compartment was by a full-width, top-hinged bootlid which was self-supporting in the open position. An unobstructed false floor was positioned above the spare wheel; thus allowing the latter to be brought into use without disturbing any luggage. Beneath the compartment, and well protected by the chassis members, was the petrol tank of a particularly useful 15 gallons capacity.

The modest overall length already referred to, was, in conjunction with a wheelbase of only 7 feet 10 inches, a factor which meant that in order to provide adequate knee room for the rear seat passengers, the seat itself was placed between the rear wheels with its backrest right over the rear axle line. This intrusion of the rear wheel arches into the passenger space resulted in a rear seat width which, at 43 inches, was somewhat narrow in a car of 5 feet 9 inches overall width. In the front however, the situation was far more satisfactory, with an uninterrupted cushion width of 55 inches making three-abreast seating a comfortable proposition.

Good quality materials, and a high standard of finish was evident throughout the interior furnishings, with leather upholstery and fitted carpets giving a luxury image. The front doors featured swivelling quarter windows, and trims which included usefully sized "pull out" pockets. Noteworthy also were window winders with spring loaded handles which lay flat against the doors when not in use, likewise, the twin sun visors were also recessed into the roof lining when not required.

Facing the driver was a sprung T-spoked steering wheel

complete with a full circle chromed ring with which to operate the dual horns. The plastic facia panel featured a glovebox ahead of the passenger, and instrumentation in front of the driver consisting of oil pressure and water temperature gauges, and an electric clock, in addition to the usual speedometer and fuel contents gauge.

As first announced, the pushrod-operated overhead valve engine which was to power the Vanguard was of 1849cc, this capacity being arrived at by way of an 80mm diameter bore and a stroke of 92mm. However, an increase in the bore measurement to 85mm was made within only a matter of months after production was underway, and, as far as can be ascertained, before any Vanguards had been delivered in the home market. This change resulted in a much more useful capacity of 2088cc. A single Solex downdraught carburettor supplied the mixture, and on a compression ratio of 6.7:1 the unit now developed 68bhp at 4200rpm, with a corresponding torque figure of 108lbs/ft at 2000rpm. This engine, which was being shared in substantially similar form with the Ferguson tractor which Standard were producing under licence at that time, was of a particularly robust construction. Perhaps the most notable feature was the use of easily replaceable "wet" cylinder liners, so called because their outside circumference formed the inside of the water jacketing, an arrangement which, in addition to giving ample water circulation around each cylinder for even cooling, also had the rather more obvious advantage of eliminating the necessity to rebore if and when an overhaul became necessary. The three main bearing crankshaft featured main and big end bearing journals of a diameter which allowed substantial overlap despite the relatively long throw associated with the 92mm stroke.

Mated to this engine, via a mechanically operated clutch, was a three-speed gearbox complete with synchromesh between all gears. The ratios were selected by a steering column-mounted lever which was situated on the right – or offside – of the car, an arrangement apparently chosen to facilitate three abreast seating in the front compartment. Completing the transmission were an open propeller shaft and a hypoid rear axle assembly with a ratio of 4.625:1, which, in conjunction with 5.50 x 16 tyres gave overall gearing of 16.5mph per 1000rpm.

Independent front suspension was of the coil and wishbone variety, whilst at the rear the live axle was located by longitudinally mounted semi-elliptic leaf springs. Anti roll bars were employed at both front and rear to keep body roll within reasonable limits during cornering. A steering box of the Bishop cam and roller type was situated ahead of the front axle line, from where it controlled the direction of the front wheels via a three piece track rod layout. Rather curiously in view of the 16 inch roadwheels, the all hydraulic braking system featured drums of only 9 inches diameter, these containing shoes which gave a total lining area of 119 square inches, a somewhat marginal figure for a car with a kerb weight of 25cwt, and an 80mph potential.

Almost all the Vanguard production went overseas during the first two years or so, and it was not until 1950 that the model began to appear in significant numbers on the roads of Britain. By this time, a very roomy estate car had been added to the range, and the Vanguard was also displaying some minor changes. Separate sidelights beneath the headlights were now incorporated in the front

Overleaf, left. No outrageous claims in this low key contemporary advertisement. The smooth lines of the early Vanguard are captured well in this period piece for the Standard Motor Company featuring their "world" car.

Overleaf, right. A bonnet motif, separate sidelights, and rear wheelarch spats identified the 1950 Standard Vanguard. This is another contemporary advertisement.

127

WE BRITISH engineering craftsmen have always been proud of our skill—but as things are today we can't afford to live on our past achievements. We've got to harness our skill to new and bolder methods of production. In the Standard Motor Company Organisation we know what that means. A new car designed for the world—the Standard Vanguard. Good to drive, good to look at. A single model produced in a plant so planned that alternative types of engine—to power either car or tractor—are being manufactured from the same machine tools; bodies and chassis assembled with the minimum of labour wastage; workers' incentives increased by a new bonus system; production target placed at 500 cars a day. So there it is—one car, one plan, one target. The result—a product which is adding new honours to British engineering craftsmanship all over the world.

The STANDARD Vanguard

STANDARD VANGUARD

The Family Car—
popular everywhere

THE STANDARD MOTOR COMPANY LTD., COVENTRY

London: 37, Davies St., Grosvenor Square, W.1.   Tel: May. 5011

STANDARD CARS · STANDARD COMMERCIAL VEHICLES · FERGUSON TRACTORS · TRIUMPH CARS

All that's best in Britain...

wings, and a bonnet motif had also made an appearance. The doors did not now reach down to the extreme lower edge of the bodywork, terminating instead just above a new sill panel. Rear wheel spats, their bottom edges moulded to match the sill, gave a sleeker look to the car as a whole. An increase in tyre size to 5.75 x 16 raised the gearing to 17mph per 1000rpm, and inside, the steering column gearchange lever was now in the conventional position on the left – or nearside – of the column. A basic version of the car, with vinyl upholstery and without a heater, was now available at £658, whilst a very fully-equipped model, with heater, radio, leather, and an overdrive, also represented good value at £765. The Laycock de Normanville overdrive was a factory fitted option only and was making its first appearance on an inexpensive British car. Arranged to operate on top gear only on the Vanguard, engagement of the overdrive was by bringing the gearchange lever towards the driver when in the top gear position – a simple fingertip operation.

The performance of the Vanguard included a maximum speed approaching 80mph, and a rate of acceleration which would take it from rest to 60mph in around 25 seconds. This was accompanied by an overall fuel consumption which would usually be in the 22/23mpg range, good figures for a 2.1-litre 25cwt car, and which could be further improved upon by some 3/4mpg if the overdrive was specified.

Being seated directly above the axle, the rear seat passengers did not enjoy quite so good a ride as did those in front, although by

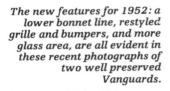

The new features for 1952: a lower bonnet line, restyled grille and bumpers, and more glass area, are all evident in these recent photographs of two well preserved Vanguards.

overall standards the Vanguard rode well. Roadholding which was certainly adequate would nevertheless have been better with rather more ample tyres than the 5.75 section covers used. However, although considerable roll could be induced during decidedly brisk cornering, the general handling qualities complemented the performance sufficiently enough to ensure that good cross country averages were usually within the Vanguard's reach, and taken as a whole its performance and 'roadability' set quite high standards in its class.

Several styling changes were introduced in October 1951, by which time – largely due to purchase tax increases – the price of the basic Vanguard had risen to £919. A new bonnet now gave the car a lower frontal appearance, and was accompanied by a re-designed grille with an oblong chromed surround and central horizontal bar. New bumpers and over-riders were introduced, that at the front still housing the oblong number plate. At the rear, however, the number plate was now of a square shape and mounted centrally on the bootlid where, unfortunately, it now looked like an afterthought. Two worthwhile changes at the rear were the introduction of a much wider window, and the concealing of the petrol filler cap in the nearside wing behind a flush fitting panel.

After more than five years of production, during which time only very minor changes in specification had been made, an extensively redesigned Phase II Vanguard was announced early in 1953. Although the front end of the car – including the by now rather dated "vee" windscreen – remained substantially as before, from the centre pillars which were moved back slightly, allowing wider front doors, the rear bodywork was entirely new.

The principal change was the elimination of the "beetle back" that had characterised the car so far, this being replaced by a new stepped rear end structure which now gave the Vanguard the "three box" shape that was already well established elsewhere. Although this design eliminated the six side window arrangement, thanks to wider rear doors the new rear quarter pillars were quite slim and, as this was accompanied by a further useful increase in the rear screen width, rearward vision was in fact greatly improved.

The interior arrangements and dimensions were virtually unchanged, but ease of entry and exit was notably improved by the increase in front and rear door width of 3 and 5 inches, respectively. The re-designed boot housed a new 12 gallon fuel tank in a transverse position behind the rear seat, whilst the spare wheel now resided underneath the car in the space vacated by the original tank.

Numerous small changes were introduced into the mechanical specification. The clutch was now hydraulically activated, and an increase in the engine's compression ratio to 7.2:1 promised a slight improvement in acceleration in conjunction with the use of Premium grade petrol. Variable rate springs at the rear increased the roll stiffness slightly and resulted in the deletion of the rear anti roll bar, whilst roadholding was further improved by the adoption of 6.00 x 16 tyres on wider rims than before. The Vanguard was now considerably updated, and as the improvements were introduced without any increase in price the Phase II model was obviously well placed to maintain the market share which the earlier car had established.

In February 1954 the Standard Motor Company became the

Perfect Control

You'll find the Standard Vanguard a pleasure to drive even under the most trying conditions. With its exceptional road-holding qualities and positive steering the strain on long journeys is reduced to a minimum. For easy control the instruments are carefully grouped in front of the driver and can be read at a glance day or night. At the touch of your foot the accelerator brings the smooth 2 litre engine leaping into life, providing an ample reserve of power for all occasions.

THE STANDARD VANGUARD

The world's most experienced car

PRICE **£555** (P.T. £232.7.6.)

Photographed in 1980, this well preserved Phase II model looks all set to give many more years of faithful service.

The facia layout of the Phase II model was similar to the earlier cars. A slight frontal change was the widened grille now encompassing the sidelights.

THE STANDARD VANGUARD

...restyled for tomorrow's needs

Arriving early in 1953, the Phase II model featured completely redesigned rear-end bodywork which successfully up-dated the car's appearance. Again in this advertisement Standard make very modest claims compared to the hyperbole used by some of their competitors.

★ 80 M.P.H. ★ SEATS SIX IN COMFORT ★ 2 LITRE ENGINE ★ HYDRAULICALLY OPERATED CLUTCH
★ LARGE WRAP-ROUND REAR WINDOW ★ STIFFENED REAR SUSPENSION FOR ROAD HOLDING
★ 24 M.P.G. ★ RUSTPROOFED BODY ★ CAPACIOUS LUGGAGE BOOT ★ SWIFT ACCELERATION

£590 (P.T. £246 19s. 2d.) *Radio, Heater and Overdrive are optional extras.*

first in Britain to offer a production diesel-engined car, with the announcement that the Vanguard was now available with a compression ignition engine of the company's own design. Although of almost identical cubic capacity – 2092cc – the diesel engine was in fact a different unit altogether from the Vanguard's petrol engine, its somewhat massive structure adding a further 2cwt to the car's unladen weight, and this factor, coupled with only 40bhp at 3000rpm resulted in a meagre performance by comparison with the petrol-engined car.

Although available on the home market, at £1099, the Vanguard Diesel was intended primarily for those countries where fuel oil was taxed far less than was the case in Britain, and with its 50 plus mpg potential at 40mph it would also be particularly useful on long range sorties in sparsely populated territories. The Phase II model continued in production until late in 1955, when it was replaced by the Phase III model, the major feature of which was a completely new bodyshell of monocoque construction.

Datapanel: Standard Vanguard Phase I/II

Standard Vanguard Phase I/II

Engine	*4 cyl, ohv*
Capacity	*2088cc*
Bore	*85mm*
Stroke	*92mm*
Compression ratio	*6.7:1 (7.2:1 Phase II)*
Max BHP	*68 @ 4200rpm*
Max torque	*108lbs/ft @ 2000rpm*
Gearing	*16.9mph/1000rpm (17.2mph/1000 Phase II)*
Tyres	*5.75 x 16 (6.00 x 16 Phase II)*
Kerb weight	*25 1/4cwt*
Overall length	*13ft 8in (14ft Phase II)*
Overall width	*5ft 9in*
Wheelbase	*7ft 10in*

Performance/Phase 1 (overdrive)

"The Autocar"
road tests 1952

Max speed:	
Measured in o/drive	*77.5mph (mean)*
	81.5mph (best)
2nd gear	*57mph*
1st gear	*26mph*
Acceleration:	
0-30mph	*6.5 seconds*
0-50mph	*15.8 seconds*
0-60mph	*24.5 seconds*
0-70mph	*39.7 seconds*
	Overdrive/Top gear/2nd gear
20-40mph	*16.4/11.4/7.0 seconds*
30-50mph	*16.9/12.2/10.0 seconds*
40-60mph	*22.7/15.0/– seconds*
Fuel consumption	*27.6 mpg (470 miles)*

Chapter 6
Standard

Eight/Ten/Pennant

The Standard Motor Company abandoned its "one model" policy (the 2.1-litre Vanguard being the only model listed between 1948-53) early in 1952 at which time development work began on a completely new economy car.

Unveiled in September 1953, the new Standard Eight was launched into direct competition with the well established Morris Minor and Austin A30. Despite very compact dimensions, 11 feet 11 inches long with a width of 4 feet 10 inches, the bodyshell featured four doors, and indeed, rather surprisingly for this end of the market, a two door version was never to go on sale. Of monocoque construction, the body was almost wholly a stressed skin structure: two different skin thicknesses being used depending upon the load. A transverse stiffener was welded into the front bulkhead, whilst box section stiffeners ran behind the sill area and over the rear axle. A detachable subframe consisting of longerons and a front crossmember carried the engine and front suspension mounting points. This subframe also carried the front bumper attachment points, and as all

This early advertisement captures the chunky, but very neat, lines of the Standard Eight accurately, although the same cannot be said about the relative size of the people! The hubcaps were, in fact, an optional extra and the advertisement seeks to make a virtue of the fact that there was no external access to the boot!

the car for
the family

The Standard Eight possesses all those features that make it the ideal family car. Fuel consumption of 45.55 m.p.g. cuts running costs to a minimum; the roomy interior — seating four with ease — with four large doors — ensures comfort on the longest journey; the roomy dust and rain sealed boot will take all the luggage; the lively 803 cc. engine provides smooth effortless running while the hydraulic brakes and independent front suspension ensure perfect road holding and ease of control on the roughest roads.

Price £339 *(P.T. £142.7.6)*

Make a date with

THE STANDARD EIGHT

four wings were also detachable the new Standard offered considerable convenience by comparison with some models should accident repairs become necessary.

Access to the luggage compartment was unusual, being via the split, pull down backrests of the rear passenger seat. The two halves of the backrest could be folded independently, an arrangement which would allow quite bulky objects to be carried whilst still leaving room for one rear seat passenger. A 7 gallon fuel tank was situated in the nearside rear, its filler cap protruding from the side rear bodywork just above the wing. The only external access at the rear was a small cover which concealed the spare wheel, this item residing horizontally beneath the boot floor.

At the front, access to the engine bay was by a wide rear hinged bonnet. Beneath the front of this, the air intake for the radiator was simply an aperture in the front panel, devoid of the usual grille, with chrome plated bumpers, door handles and lamp surrounds being the extent of bright metal decoration.

The simple instrumentation allowed useful facia stowage space, whilst at the rear the fold-forward seat arrangement catered for large amounts of luggage when necessary. The sliding windows, simple door catches, and untrimmed doors are all evident in these views.

FEATURES OF THE NEW STANDARD EIGHT

Driving seat and controls. The two-spoked steering wheel allows an uninterrupted view of the instruments.

FEATURES OF THE NEW STANDARD EIGHT

Unique luggage space, showing the large amount of luggage that can be stowed when the car is travelling with only a driver and passenger.

An appreciably better equipped de luxe model appeared in May 1954.

—and now it's de luxe!

The Standard Eight de luxe has winding windows, Vynide upholstery, push-button door locks, twin sun visors, hub caps, etc. There is a lively 803 cc. engine with its 45/55 miles per gallon that keeps costs down to a minimum; four doors for easy access; large rain and dust proof luggage boot; hydraulic brakes; independent front suspension for perfect road holding and easy steering on the roughest roads — features that make this fine car the world's best value in motoring to-day.

Price £379 (P.T. £159.0.10)
Basic Model £339
(P.T. £142.7.6)

STANDARD EIGHT *de luxe*

THE STANDARD MOTOR CO. LTD., COVENTRY, ENGLAND
London Showrooms: 15-17 Berkeley Square, W.1. Telephone: Grosvenor 8181

Inside, the trim level was consistent with the economy image. The doors were fully recessed and without window winding mechanism, a horizontal sliding arrangement being used. The simple tubular steel seats featured tension springs, and were upholstered in Tygan, whilst a rubber covering sufficed for the floor. Facing the driver was a single circular instrument housing which consisted of a speedometer and fuel gauge only, these being viewed through the upper half of the two spoke steering wheel. All three pedals were of the pendant type, and the standard equipment included a single windscreen wiper and sunvisor – with these items being available for the front seat passenger at extra cost – and semaphore type direction indicators.

The power unit was a new pushrod operated ohv four-cylinder engine with a bore and stroke of 58mm x 76mm giving a capacity of 803cc, identical measurements in fact to the rival BMC A-series unit. A Solex downdraught carburettor supplied the mixture,

The Ten also arrived in May 1954, and was equipped to the de luxe level from the start. The opening rear boot, although depicted here, did not in fact appear until some time later!

THE STANDARD TEN

The Standard Ten provides comfort for the particular, economy for the careful—petrol consumption is 45/50 miles per gallon—while the lively 948 cc. engine has an ample reserve of power for every purpose. You will find, too, in the Standard Ten such acceptable amenities as adjustable front seats, a large luggage boot, press-button door handles, plus a surprising roominess inside.

PRICE **£409** (P.T. £171 . 10 . 10)

and with a compression ratio of 7.25:1 the engine developed 26bhp at 4500rpm with 40lbs/ft torque at 2800rpm. The $6\frac{1}{4}$ inch diameter clutch was activated hydraulically, and the four-speed gearbox featured synchromesh between the three upper ratios, the selection of

A 1956 advertisement announcing the optional "Standrive" two-pedal control.

and now

STANDRIVE

Incorporating Newtondrive Patents

Two-Pedal Control

Standrive two-pedal control is now available on the Standard Super Ten and the Standard Ten Companion as an optional extra. Standrive provides the driver with all the advantages of an automatic clutch, enabling a clutchless gear change to be made. It permits leisurely change of gear or, when desired, a rapid shift into higher or lower ratios with equal smoothness and precision.

THE STANDARD MOTOR COMPANY LTD., COVENTRY, ENGLAND

London Showrooms : 15-17 Berkeley Square, W.1.   Tel : Grosvenor 8181

STANDARD CARS · TRIUMPH CARS · STANDARD COMMERCIAL VEHICLES · STANDARD DIESEL ENGINES · FERGUSON TRACTORS

which was by a long, direct-acting floor-mounted lever. The first gear ratio was deliberately extremely low, its function being to ensure that the car would start comfortably from rest on a gradient of 1 in 4 when carrying four adults. This requirement was said at the time to be the prime reason for adopting a four-speed arrangement on this economy model. An open propeller shaft took the drive to a hypoid bevel rear axle with a ratio of 4.875:1, which gave overall gearing of 13.3mph per 1000rpm in conjunction with 5.20 x 13 tyres.

A Burman steering box was mounted ahead of the axle line, and the independent front suspension units consisted of double wishbones, coil springs and hydraulic shock absorbers. The rear springs were longitudinally mounted, each featuring four leaves and passing over the rear axle to which they were attached by the usual U-bolts. A Girling hydraulic braking system was employed, and consisted of 7 inch diameter drums on all four wheels, with a brake shoe width of $1\frac{1}{4}$ inches giving a total lining area of 68 square inches. The cable-operated handbrake featured a pull-up lever conveniently situated between the front seats.

At a tax paid price of £481, the new Standard Eight was an attractive newcomer to the economy end of the market. Its performance, with a maximum speed of 62/63mph, a 0-60mph time of around 50 seconds and a 50mpg plus economy potential being broadly comparable with its most obvious well established rival, the Austin A30 which was now listed at £504 in four door configuration.

In May 1954, a De-Luxe model was made available. Priced at £538, the De-Luxe car featured Vynide upholstery, twin sunvisors and twin windscreen wipers. All four doors were fully trimmed and received wind-up windows, whilst the roadwheels now came complete with chrome plated hubcaps. At the same time, a Standard Ten also made its appearance, trimmed to the De-Luxe specification and priced at £580. The principle new feature of the Ten was, of course, the engine. An increase in bore size to 63mm was made possible by siamesing the bores in pairs, and this resulted in a useful capacity increase to 948cc from which 35bhp was now developed. An axle ratio of 4.55:1 was accompanied by 5.60 x 13 tyres, thus raising the overall gearing to 15mph per 1000rpm. All of this resulted in a maximum speed which could exceed 65mph, allied to a 0-60mph capability of around 36 seconds. An overall fuel consumption of approximately 40mpg kept the Ten comfortably in the economy class.

An estate car, the Standard Ten Companion, made its appearance in October 1954, priced at £652. Structurally, the front end of the Companion was identical to that of the saloon, and the saloon rear wing design was also retained. The rear passenger doors had squared-up window frames, and the windows themselves were fixed in these doors as were those in the rear quarters. The roofline continued horizontally to the end of the car, with access to the loading area being via two van-type doors; both of which were fitted with over-centre stays to hold them in the open position. Folding the rear seat squab forward automatically lowered the seat cushion, thus bringing the folded squab down to the rear floor level. The back of the squab was covered in the same rubber material as the loading area floor.

In June 1955 the basic Eight was improved by the addition of fully trimmed doors, these now also being complete with window winding mechanism and push-button handles. The model was now to be known as the Standard Family Eight, and was priced at £509. The De-Luxe model now acquired leather upholstery and could be distinguished externally by the introduction of a chromium radiator grille. These improvements resulted in a new price for the De-Luxe of £537. Improvements at the same time to the estate car included winding windows in the rear passenger doors, whilst the whole range now benefited from the introduction of self-cancelling flashing indicators.

Early in 1956 the De-Luxe models became known as the Super Eight (£608) and Super Ten (£646), whilst a Family Ten (£614) was made available for those drivers wishing for the Ten's performance but without the higher trim level, or the opening bootlid which was at last making an appearance, but on the Super Ten only.

The small Standards had earned an excellent reputation for roadworthiness, and indeed, a Ten with a highly modified engine had scored a notable outright victory in the 1955 RAC Rally. Tuning specialists, Alexander Engineering, were now offering an engine conversion for the Ten. This consisted of a modified cylinder head which gave a compression ratio of 8.25:1, stronger valve springs, twin SU carburettors and a four branch exhaust manifold. Priced at £43, this conversion raised the power output to approximately 45bhp at 5500rpm and enabled the Ten to reach 60mph from rest in 22/23 seconds on its way to a maximum of almost 80mph. Alexander could also supply a front anti-roll torsion bar, which, at the expense of a slightly firmer ride, would further enhance the Standard's already very good handling characteristics. The Standard Motor Company approved of the conversion to such an extent that a new car so fitted did not have its warranty invalidated, a fact which speaks very well indeed of the manufacturer's confidence in the ruggedness of the basic engine.

Two pedal control, based on the Newtondrive solenoid operated/centrifugal clutch arrangement, but in this instance known as "Standrive" became available as an extra cost option late in 1956.

By early 1957 the range was into Phase II configuration, improved trim, including carpeting and two tone seating in the more expensive models being the principal new features. The most

The rear-end styling of the small Standards gave a good visual balance to the model as a whole. Depicted here is a later example with the opening boot lid.

8 *plus* features on the NEW Standard 8

PRICE · £410 (P.T. £206.7.0) TOTAL: £616.7.0

PLUS new-opening rear boot
with 12 to 38 cu. ft. of luggage space

PLUS new frontal grille
PLUS new deep-pile carpet
PLUS new bright interior fittings

PLUS new interior light
PLUS new luxury trim
PLUS new Standard economy

and new Gold Star 803 c.c. Power Plus engine

for double life and brisker performance

The only 8 h.p. 4 door saloon made in the U.K.   Twelve months guarantee
THE STANDARD MOTOR COMPANY LTD., COVENTRY, ENGLAND   London Showrooms: 15-17 Berkeley Sq. W.1

The exclusive car of the year

Exciting new body lines with wide choice of two-tone colour schemes.

Luxurious interior fittings including the new self-breathing Vynair upholstery.

Sports car-type remote control, floor mounted gear lever.

Super power Gold Star engine of 948 c.c. giving 42/47 m.p.g.

Standrive Two-Pedal Control and Laycock Overdrive available as optional extras.

The New Standard   PENNANT

Price: £485 Plus P.T. £243.17.0

expensive Eight now also featured the external bootlid. A further transmission option was the Laycock overdrive. Priced at £63, the overdrive added some 10% to the total price, but did offer a useful potential fuel saving on top of the already impressive mpg figures which the small Standards could achieve. Raising the overall gearing to 17.5mph per 1000rpm on the Eight, and to 20mph per 1000rpm on the Ten, the overdrive offered remarkably relaxed cruising by small car standards, and as it also operated on second and third gear, the driver had a choice of no less than seven ratios! ''Gold Star'' engines, with a raised compression ratio were also now a feature of both the Eight and the Ten.

An additional, top of the range model – the Pennant – was introduced in October 1957. External recognition features included new front wings with a hooded headlamp treatment, a mildly finned effect above the rear wings, two tone paintwork, a full width radiator grille, chrome side mouldings and a larger rear window. The re-designed interior boasted a new facia with a leathercloth top, two circular instrument dials facing the driver, and on the passenger's side a glove compartment complete with a lockable lid. Hard wearing leathercloth was also used on the seat facings, which, like the door trims were finished in a dual tone scheme. Power for the Pennant came from a ''Gold Star'' Ten engine. These units, which were recognizable by their gold coloured rocker covers, now also benefited from the introduction of a higher lift camshaft, and on the Pennant a larger carburettor. Gear selection on the Pennant was by a short remote-type floor-mounted lever. Variable rate rear springs were a Pennant feature which were also being adopted by the Eight and Ten. Priced at £728, the Pennant was the highest priced of the small cars

This is the Wilding family's early 1955 De Luxe Standard Eight during a summer holiday in the 'fifties. The picturesque setting is below Kilnsey Craig, near Kettlewell, Yorkshire. (Courtesy Chris Wilding).

available at that time, but was offering a distinctive appearance and a high trim level for this class of car.

The Family and Super designations had been deleted from the Eight earlier in the year, leaving just one model which was known as the Gold Star Eight, at £638. The Ten now followed suit, with just the Gold Star model being listed at £653. The Ten Companion at £743 also now came with the Gold Star engine.

The range continued virtually unchanged until the summer of 1959, when, in May, the Pennant was deleted. The Eight and Ten saloons were discontinued in July, the small Standards having given way to the Triumph Herald, which, apart from the 948cc engine was an almost totally new car. The Standard Ten Companion, now with Pennant type grille and front wings, continued in production, finally being replaced by the Herald estate car in 1961.

Datapanel: Standard Eight/Ten

	Eight	Ten
Engine	4 cyl, ohv	4 cyl, ohv
Capacity	803cc	948cc
Bore	58mm	63mm
Stroke	76mm	76mm
Compression ratio	7.25:1	7.0:1
Max BHP	26 @ 4500rpm	33 @ 4500rpm
Max torque	39lbs/ft @ 2800rpm	46lbs/ft @ 2500rpm
Gearing	13.3mph/1000rpm	15mph/1000rpm
Tyres	5.20 x 13	5.60 x 13
Kerb weight	14cwt	14.5cwt
Overall length	11ft 10in	11ft 10in
Overall width	4ft 10in	4ft 10in
Wheelbase	7ft	7ft

Performance

	"The Autocar" 17th May 1957	"The Autocar" 29th March 1957
Max speed:		
Top gear	62.2mph (mean)	65.0mph (mean)
	65.0mph (best)	65.5mph (best)
3rd gear	58mph	58mph
2nd gear	34mph	38mph
1st gear	20mph	22mph
Acceleration:		
0-30mph	8.2 seconds	8.1 seconds
0-50mph	24.5 seconds	23.3 seconds
0-60mph	54.4 seconds	38.1 seconds
	Top gear/3rd gear	Top gear/3rd gear
20-40mph	18.0/11.6 seconds	15.6/10.7 seconds
30-50mph	21.3/25.9 seconds	18.9/14.1 seconds
40-60mph	–/– seconds	28.5/– seconds
Fuel consumption	44mpg (128 miles)	40.5mpg (390 miles)

Chapter 6
Standard

Vanguard Phase III/ Sportsman/ Ensign/ Vignale

In October 1955, the familiar Standard Vanguard, which, even in its Phase II configuration was beginning to look rather dated, gave way to the Phase III model in which the principal change was a completely new integrally constructed bodyshell.

Substantial chassis type members were welded into the structure at both front and rear, each terminating where they met with similar transverse stiffeners under the floor. The transverse sections were tied into the sill structure, and the bottom end rigidity of the structure as a whole was such as to suggest that perhaps a convertible model would follow, although in the event this was not to be the case.

The considerable glass area included a full width rear window which left only narrow rear quarter pillars, and a notable feature of the four front-hinged doors was that their steel construction terminated at window sill level, with the window frames themselves being of extruded aluminium with an anodized surface. Of narrow section, these frames allowed a large side window area and also offered a useful weight saving. The full width bonnet was self-supporting, whilst at the rear the bootlid was held in the open position by means of a ratchet type stay. The $12\frac{1}{2}$ gallon fuel tank – complete with a lockable filler cap – was situated behind the rear seat; and beneath the wide, flat boot floor resided the spare wheel. When required, the spare had to be lowered by a hoist operated by the starting handle. When not in use the starting handle and wheel changing tools were stored in a hinged tray above the fuel tank.

Bright metal embellishment was confined to the simple grille surround, headlamp and rear lamp rims, bootlid hinges, door handles, bumpers – complete with over-riders, hubcaps and screen surrounds, and the car's appearance as a whole was clean and uncluttered.

The new Phase III Vanguard featured a completely new integrally constructed bodyshell which housed similar mechanical components to the previous model. These are contemporary press release photographs.

RHP 555

An increase in the wheelbase of 8 inches over the previous model provided a much improved layout in so far as the rear seat passengers were concerned. Both the full-width bench seats were upholstered in vynide, and both featured pull-down centre armrests. All four doors were equipped with armrest/doorpulls, and each also featured window winding mechanism and swivelling quarter windows. Facing the driver was a two-spoked steering wheel with a half horn ring, and a neat and comprehensive instrument panel. Gauges for fuel level, oil pressure, water temperature, and an ammeter were in a row beneath an arc shaped speedometer. Pendant foot pedals for the clutch and brakes were an up-to-date feature, as were flashing indicators. A heating and de-misting unit, and electric screenwashers were standard equipment.

Residing under the bonnet was the well-proven 2088cc unit of the earlier Vanguard, still rated at 68bhp at 4200rpm and 108lbs/ft torque at 2000rpm. The engine cooling arrangements, however, now differed from the previous model, with the adoption of a wide crossflow radiator; an arrangement chosen in this instance to allow a low bonnet line. The all-synchromesh three-speed gearbox, with column-mounted change mechanism was also as before, with the Laycock overdrive continuing to be an optional extra fitting. A new axle ratio of 4.3:1 raised the overall gearing to 18mph per 1000rpm, a desirable change made possible by the fact that the integral construction had resulted in a weight saving of almost 2cwt, and so the engine could now pull a usefully higher and more economical gear without loss of acceleration.

The coil and wishbone independent front suspension units were part of a separate sub-assembly which included a very substantial crossmember: this being bolted to two re-inforced attachment points on each side of the front lower bodywork. Also attached to this crossmember was the forward mounted Burman recirculating ball steering box which controlled the direction of the front wheels via a three piece track rod. Longitudinally mounted leaf springs located the live rear axle, and the Lockheed hydraulic braking system, with its 9 inch diameter and 121 square inch lining area was similar to that of the previous Vanguard. Also as before were the 16 inch diameter road wheels, but surprisingly now shod with tyres of only 5.50 section.

With a maximum speed of almost exactly 80mph and the ability to reach 70mph from rest in around 37/38 seconds the Phase III model had a similar performance to that of the previous model, but the higher overall gearing and lighter weight resulted in this being accompanied by a worthwhile improvement in fuel economy with overall journey figures in the 27/28mpg range being easily attainable. The general ride and handling qualities also showed an improvement, the lower centre of gravity resulting in rather less lean during fast cornering despite the absence now of anti-roll bars.

Priced at £849, the Phase III Vanguard was faced with stiff opposition from the Austin Westminster De-Luxe, £834; Vauxhall Cresta, £844; and Ford Zodiac, £851. All three of these cars were offering rather more speed and acceleration in addition to the superior mechanical refinement usually associated with in-line 6-cylinder engines, whilst the Cresta, and particularly the Zodiac, were also more comprehensively equipped. However, the Vanguard was to prove to be a worthy contender, holding its own very well in this price

Distinctive frontal treatment identified the higher powered Sportsman here featured in a Laycock de Normanville advertisement.

The lower powered, and less expensive Ensign, was also identified externally by frontal styling treatment.

standard equipment on the

STANDARD VANGUARD *Sportsman*

Laycock DE NORMANVILLE *Overdrive*

and available on over 30 other British cars

This further example of the growing appreciation, by manufacturers and public alike, of the exclusive advantages of the Laycock Overdrive is a tribute to ALL-BRITISH design and engineering skill. In addition to the SPORTSMAN, the Laycock Overdrive is available on—Sunbeam Rapier, Rover, Austin-Healey, Triumph T.R.3, Vanguard III, Sapphire 236, three Jaguar models, and many other famous British cars.

category, and certainly more than just continuing to please those who had been well served by the previous models.

The range multiplied in August 1956 with the announcement of the Vanguard Sportsman. As its name suggested, the Sportsman was a high performance edition of the Vanguard, offering a useful increase in both speed and acceleration. Although of the same capacity, the Sportsman's engine differed in several important respects from that in the basic model, and incorporated features of the 1991cc derivative of this unit which powered the company's Triumph TR3 sports car. The power and torque outputs, 90bhp at 4500rpm and 121lbs/ft at 2500rpm, were arrived at by increasing the compression ratio to 8.0:1, replacing the single Solex with twin SU carburettors, and fitting triple valve springs. Increased strength came from adopting the longer cylinder head bolts, stiffened connecting rods, and lead indium bearings of the TR3, along with improved Vanguard pistons. The overdrive, operating on second and top gear, was to be a standard feature of the Sportsman's specification in conjunction with a lower rear axle ratio of 4.55:1. This arrangement giving the effect of a close ratio five speed gearbox. All of this was sufficient to put the Sportsman into the genuine 90mph category, and enabled it to accelerate from rest to 60mph and 70mph in around 18 and 26 seconds, respectively. An increase in brake drum diameter to 10 inches, in conjunction with wider shoes gave the very ample lining area of 175 square inches with which to tame the increased speed, whilst an anti-roll bar introduced between the front lower wishbones kept the cornering capabilities in line with the performance increase. Identifying the Sportsman externally was a new grille of rather more traditional radiator-shape, deeper bumpers and over-riders, and a two tone paint finish. The interior boasted two tone hide, or a hide and cloth combination for the upholstery, a cigar lighter, and an electric clock.

Completing the range now, came the Phase III Estate. Based closely on the saloon, the estate car bodywork retained the rear passenger doors, rear wings and tail light treatment. Access to the new loading area was through a horizontally split tailgate, the upper half of which featured a large window and was arranged to lift upwards. The lower tailgate was hinged at the bottom and featured an internal lidded compartment in which the tool kit was housed. A wide, flat 14 gallon fuel tank was situated beneath the rear floor, with its lockable filler cap concealed behind a hinged flap in the nearside rear wing. Beneath the tank was the spare wheel on a hinged tray. A technical change now was that some of the cars would be fitted with a cam and roller steering box, by Cam Gears Ltd, as an alternative to that supplied by Burman. Which type was fitted depended solely upon the supply position as the car left the line. The price of the saloon had by this time risen to £899, the estate car was introduced at £1148, with the top of the range Sportsman being listed at £1231.

The range diversified further one year later, when, in October 1957, the Ensign saloon was announced. Essentially a de-trimmed Vanguard, the Ensign was identified by a simple mesh grille, painted headlamp surrounds and lack of over-riders. Inside, the bench seats and doors were without armrests, and the only instrument in addition to the speedometer was the fuel gauge. However, the pvc trim material was in bright dual tones and as a result the interior scene did not in fact seem unduly austere. Power for the Ensign came from a similar unit to the Vanguard, but with a narrower bore of 76mm reducing the capacity to 1670cc from which 60bhp was developed. Mated to this engine was a four-speed gearbox with a long floor-mounted lever, which still allowed three abreast seating in the front, and with intelligently chosen ratios that would ensure an entirely adequate performance from the smaller engined car. A 0-60mph time of approximately 26 seconds and a maximum speed just in excess of 75mph were accompanied by an overall fuel consumption in the 28/30mpg region. At £899, the Ensign was a tempting proposition to those who found the Vanguard – by this time priced at £1013 – just a little out of reach. A worthwhile improvement throughout the range at this time was the adoption of slightly smaller, 15 inch diameter roadwheels with larger section – 5.90 – tyres. Apart from this, and losing their horn ring which was replaced by a button in the steering wheel boss, the Vanguard and Sportsman continued without change to their basic specification although the four speed gearbox or a Borg Warner automatic could be ordered at extra cost now on the Vanguard only.

The rather highly-priced Sportsman was discontinued early in 1958, but the Vanguard underwent a face-lifting operation by Italian stylist Michelotti, in conjunction with specialist coachbuilders Vignale of Turin, the results of which were shown at Earls Court in October that year. To be known as the Vignale Vanguard, this latest version featured deeper front and rear screens, a new grille and front

The Vignale treatment also applied to the Vanguard estate car as shown by this Motor Show advertisement.

STANDARD TRIUMPH
AT THE MOTOR SHOW

THE SUPERLATIVE VIGNALE VANGUARD

British craftmanship and Italian artistry are brilliantly combined in the superlative Vignale Vanguard. The result — breathtaking beauty of line and outstanding performance with all the reliability of Standard engineering. The famous 2 litre power unit, fitted with the unique wet cylinder liners for longer life, gives surging power with real economy. The interior is spacious, the instruments planned for safer, at-a-glance reading, and a heater/air-conditioner is included as basic equipment. With the choice of a three-speed gearbox controlled from the steering column or a four-speed gearbox with floor lever (overdrive is an optional extra), the Vignale Vanguard Saloon and Estate Car are the world's finest value in motoring. The Vignale Vanguard Saloon £985.14.2 (inc. P.T.). The Vignale Vanguard Estate Car £1092.13.4 (inc. P.T.).

sidelamp treatment, redesigned rear light clusters, wheeltrims, and two tone paintwork. Over-riders were now an optional extra, whilst inside, the rear doors had lost their armrests. Wherever appropriate, the estate car also received the Vignale treatment.

The range continued unchanged until September 1960 when the Vignale Vanguard Six was introduced as an additional top of the range model. The new 6-cylinder engine owed nothing to the familiar 2-litre 4-cylinder unit, its origins in fact being in the diminutive 803cc Standard 8 engine introduced in 1953. Producing a 6-cylinder version of the Standard 8 block, with bore sizes increased from 58mm to 74mm whilst retaining the original 76mm stroke, resulted in a remarkably compact 1998cc 6-cylinder unit. The 803cc engine had not been designed with this sort of "stretch" in mind, and the increased bore now resulted in the cylinders being siamesed in pairs with the cooling water circulating around each pair rather than each individual cylinder. The advantage of the design however was that the overall length of the unit was only 2 inches more than the massive 4-cylinder Vanguard engine, and actually weighed $\frac{1}{2}$cwt less. Consequently, the new engine fitted easily into the Vanguard's roomy

A contemporary brochure for the Vignale points out features likely to appeal to the lady driver.

The smooth lines of the Vignale Vanguard will appeal instantly to the feminine eye. Yet it is the carefully thought out details that will win her approval. For example, the attractive range of colour combinations. Then there are the perfectly placed controls, responding to the lightest touch, and giving a feeling of confidence from the moment she sits in the driving seat. There are pivoting glass ventilators on the front doors, and an interior light above the windscreen. There is an air of graciousness about the Vignale Vanguard that she will find irresistible.

148

Italian stylist Michelotti added the styling touches which resulted in the Vignale Vanguard.

engine bay whilst lessening slightly the nose heavy bias in the front/rear weight distribution. On a compression ratio of 8.0:1, and with twin Solex carburettors, the new engine produced 80bhp at 4500rpm and 107lbs/ft torque at 2500rpm. These figures suggested a useful rather than startling increase in peformance, the improvement in this respect anyway was only regarded as a bonus, the prime reason for the 6-cylinders being the improved level of mechanical refinement. The transmission options remained as before, although the 4.55:1 axle – as used previously on the Sportsman – would now be fitted whenever the overdrive was specified. Recognizable externally only by the word ''SIX'' on the bonnet, and the script ''Vanguard 6'' on the boot, the new car featured many improvements to the interior trim. These included more deeply upholstered seats, padded facia and crushable visors, map pockets, improved switchgear and a new instrument binnacle with circular dials.

Purchase tax reductions the previous year had lowered prices generally, and at £1,021 the Vanguard Six was offering excellent value. Both 4 and 6-cylinder Vanguard estate cars were now available, and the 4-cylinder Vanguard saloon, now at £985 was remaining in production with the four-speed gearbox included in its standard specification. The Ensign, at £849 would continue to offer good value at the bottom end of the range. The Ensign was in fact deleted early in 1961, only to return a year later as a replacement for the 4-cylinder Vanguard which was now withdrawn in both saloon and estate car configuration.

The new Ensign was particularly interesting in that it featured the larger-bored 2138cc version of the big 4-cylinder "wet liner" engine which had been developed for the Triumph TR4 sports car, and was thus the largest engined model of the long running Vanguard family. Still priced at £849, the Ensign was good value in 1962, with its specification including the four-speed gearbox and 10 inch diameter front brake drums. It was also somewhat unusual in that with a maximum speed in excess of 85mph, and an ability to reach 60mph and 70mph from rest in around 18 and 27 seconds respectively, it was rather quicker than the top of the range 6-cylinder car!

The Ensign and the luxury Vanguard 6 continued in production until late in 1963 when the range was replaced by the rather more up-market Triumph 2000 which, whilst inheriting an uprated version of the Vanguard's 6-cylinder engine, was otherwise a completely different car.

Datapanel: Standard Vanguard Phase III/Sportsman/Vignale 6

	Vanguard Phase III (Sportsman)	Vanguard 6
Engine	4 cyl, ohv	6 cyl, ohv
Capacity	2088cc	1998cc
Bore	85mm	74.7mm
Stroke	92mm	76mm
Compression ratio	7.0:1 (8.0:1)	8.0:1
Max BHP	68 @ 4200rpm (90 @ 4500rpm)	80 @ 4500rpm
Max torque	108lbs/ft @ 2000rpm (121 @ 2500rpm)	107lbs/ft @ 2500rpm
Gearing	18mph/1000rpm (16.2mph/1000rpm)	16.2mph/1000rpm
Tyres	5.50 x 16	5.90 x 15
Kerb weight	24cwt	23 1/2cwt
Overall length	14ft 4in (14ft 5 1/2in)	14ft 3 1/2in
Overall width	5ft 7 1/2in	5ft 7 1/2in
Wheelbase	8ft 6in	8ft 6in

Performance

	"The Autocar" Road tests 1956	"The Autocar" Road Tests 1961
Max speed:		
O/D	79mph (mean) (86mph) 83mph (best) (90mph)	83.5mph (mean) 85mph (best)
Top gear	77mph (mean) (84mph) 80mph (best) (86mph)	82mph (mean) –
O/D 2nd gear	73mph (68mph)	70mph
2nd gear	57mph (54mph)	58mph
1st gear	29mph (26mph)	34mph
Acceleration:		
0-30mph	5.9 seconds (5.4)	5.0 seconds
0-50mph	14.6 seconds (12.2)	13.0 seconds
0-60mph	22.2 seconds (17.6)	19.7 seconds
0-70mph	38.8 seconds (25.2)	29.9 seconds
	Top gear/O/D2nd/2nd gear	Top gear/O/D2nd/2nd
20-40mph	10.7(9.1)/8.5(6.9)/ 6.9(5.7) seconds	9.4/7.4/6.0seconds
30-50mph	13.0(10.0)/10.4(8.1) (9.5 (6.7) seconds	10.7/8.2/7.2 seconds
40-60mph	16.5(11.8)/15.8(9.4) seconds	12.6/10.6/– seconds
50-70mph	–(14.0)/–(14.4)/– seconds	16.2/–/– seconds
Fuel consumption	30.8mpg (25.8mpg)	20.0mpg (1520 miles)

Performance figures in brackets are for Sportsman

Chapter 7
Vauxhall

Wyvern/Velox L-Series

Vauxhall's L-Series Wyvern (4-cylinder) and Velox (6-cylinder), the restyled and more powerful replacements for what was still basically their pre-war range were announced in August 1948. The passenger carrying centre section of the integrally constructed bodyshell was substantially that of the earlier cars, but to which was now added a completely restyled front and rear end.

The new front end consisted of a rear-hinged bonnet which still included the famous Vauxhall flutes, and front wings which now featured built-in combined head and sidelamp units. Finishing the front end off visually was a new low-set grille of horizontal chrome slats, and a wrap-around chrome plated bumper; whilst underneath was a subframe on which was mounted the engine and the front suspension units. Apart from the fact that the battery was mounted centrally on the bulkhead in such a position as to make inspection of the levels difficult, underbonnet accessibility was generally good for other routine inspections.

At the rear, the full-width bootlid was self-supporting, and when opened revealed a usefully large compartment. The spare wheel, however, was carried horizontally on the boot floor, with no protection being provided for suitcases, etc. Beneath the luggage compartment was a 10 gallon fuel tank. A low back panel contained twin tail lights and an oblong number plate, and beneath this ran the full width bumper bar. Over-riders on both front and rear bumpers were a standard feature of the Velox only.

Access to the passenger compartment was via four doors; all of which were hinged at the centre pillar, this particular feature underlining the model's 1930s ancestry perhaps more than anything else. All four doors were equipped with balanced drop main windows, and quarter windows were fixed in the rear doors but of the swivelling type in the front compartment. The front door trims included map pockets. Despite the relatively narrow bodywork really dictating a four-seater layout, the front seat was of the bench type. Bronze coloured hide upholstery was a standard feature of the Velox, the rear seat of which was equipped with a folding central armrest, whilst the cheaper four-cylinder car had dove-grey cloth seat coverings. The simple facia contained an instrument panel immediately in front of the driver, and consisted of a circular speedometer flanked by an ammeter and fuel gauge. The panel was viewed through a sprung T-spoked wheel, the centre boss of this housing the button with which to sound the single horn. A lidded glovebox faced the passenger and both cars were equipped with twin sunvisors, and twin windscreen wipers; the latter being operated mechanically by means of a cable drive from the engine's camshaft.

Pushrod operated overhead valve engines had been a Vauxhall feature for some years before the war, and the new four- and six-cylinder units for the Wyvern and Velox continued this arrangement. With a bore and stroke of 69.5mm x 95mm the Wyvern engine had a capacity of 1442cc. The six-cylinder engine had the same bore diameter, but the crankshaft featured a slightly longer throw with a stroke of 100mm, this resulting in a total capacity of 2275cc. Both units had a single Zenith carburettor, and with compression ratios of 6.4:1 and 6.75:1 for the four- and six-cylinder units, respectively, the power outputs were 35bhp at 3600rpm and 55bhp at 3300rpm. The cooling arrangements differed with each engine, as in addition to its larger diameter fan and increased

A 1950 advertisement for the L-series Vauxhall models.

Both the Velox and Wyvern models are obtainable in scintillating metallichrome colours: blue, grey, green and fawn (Velox only).

VAUXHALL

Velox

Wyvern

$2\frac{1}{4}$ litre six cylinder. Outstanding performance with good economy. £430 plus £120 3s. 11d. P.T.

A $1\frac{1}{2}$ litre four cylinder car of outstanding economy and good performance. £375 plus £104 18s. 4d. P.T.

VAUXHALL MOTORS LIMITED, LUTON, BEDFORDSHIRE

capacity radiator, the six-cylinder engine's cooling system was also pressurised. The three speed gearbox was provided with synchromesh between the upper two ratios, and gear selection was by a column-mounted lever. An open propeller shaft transmitted the power to a spiral bevel rear axle assembly with a ratio of 4.625:1 on the Wyvern and 4.125:1 on the Velox. These ratios, in conjunction with 16 inch diameter road wheels and 5.00 and 5.25 section tyres gave overall gearing of 16.3mph per 10000rpm and 18.0mph per 1000rpm for the Wyvern and Velox, respectively.

Independent front suspension was by a combination of torsion bars, and horizontal coil springs which were enclosed in an oil bath. At the rear, the longitudinally mounted semi-elliptic leaf springs were protected by grease filled gaiters. The steering gear was of the

Three recently taken photographs of KDU 712 – an L-Series Velox in a beautifully preserved condition.

Burman Douglas screw and nut type, and a Vauxhall/Lockheed all hydraulic braking system consisting of 9 inch drums and 100 square inches of lining area completed the technical specification.

Priced at £447, the Wyvern was aimed at those motorists whose requirements were for a really comfortable four-seater and neat furnishings combined with good overall economy, rather than exceptional performance. The performance was rather modest, with a maximum speed of only 60mph, and acceleration from rest to 50mph requiring around 27 seconds. This was however coupled with good fuel economy, with well over 30mpg being obtained at a 50mph cruise, and the Wyvern was indeed an attractive proposition in its class. Much more performance was, of course, available from the Velox, its $2\frac{1}{4}$-litre engine enabling it to reach 50 and 60mph from rest in 20 and 30 seconds and attain a maximum of more than 70mph. Fuel consumption in the 25 to 30mpg range accompanied this performance, and at its tax paid price of £550 the Velox was offering the refinements always associated with six-cylinder motoring for less money than anything else on the British market at that time.

Slight changes introduced in September 1949 included improvements in the steering gear designed to reduce friction and

steering wander, the principal changes here being a new Burman worm and peg steering box, and modified kingpins which now rotated on a single hardened steel ball at their base. New road wheels of smaller diameter – 15 inches – but slightly wider and shod with 5.90 section tyres made their appearance on the Velox only. A hidden, but useful improvement was the provision of a metal shield beneath the car to protect the exposed gearchange mechanism from the effects of mud and snow. Larger headlamps and separate sidelamps were new front end identification features on these latest models. At the rear the number plate was now square and mounted high upon the boot lid, this arrangement being chosen in answer to criticism from certain overseas markets where heavy falling snow was said to settle on the rear bumper and quickly obliterate the low mounted number plate. "Metallichrome" paint finishes – other than black – were a further new feature, and inside the car the ammeter was replaced by an engine temperature gauge. The hide upholstery was now included in the Wyvern's specification, resulting in a price increase to £479 for the four-cylinder car whilst the six-cylinder model remained unchanged at £550. These useful improvements kept the Vauxhall L Series – which were only intended as interim models – more than competitive throughout 1950, the range in fact continuing in production until August 1951 when replaced by the much larger E Series models.

Datapanel: Vauxhall L-Series Wyvern/Velox

	Wyvern	Velox
Engine	4 cyl, ohv	6 cyl, ohv
Capacity	1442cc	2275cc
Bore	69.5mm	69.5mm
Stroke	95mm	100mm
Compression ratio	6.4:1	6.75:1
Max BHP	35 @ 3600rpm	54 @ 3300rpm
Gearing	16.3mph/1000rpm	18.0mph/1000rpm (18.4mph/1000rpm with 5.90 tyres)
Tyres	5.00 x 16	5.25 x 16 (5.90 x 15 later)
Kerb weight	19 1/2cwt	22cwt
Overall length	13ft 8 1/2in	13ft 8 3/4in
Overall width	5ft 2in	5ft 2in
Wheelbase	8ft 1 3/4in	8ft 1 3/4in

Performance

	"The Motor" RT No. 8/49	"The Autocar Road Tests 1951"
Max speed:		
Top gear	60.0mph (mean) 62.1mph (best)	74.0mph (mean) –
2nd gear	44mph	49mph
1st gear	20mph	23mph
Acceleration:		
0-30mph	9.9 seconds	7.4 seconds
0-50mph	27.8 seconds	19.3 seconds
0-60mph	–	30.6 seconds
	Top gear/2nd gear	Top gear/2nd gear
20-40mph	14.5/12.2 seconds	11.8/7.7 seconds
30-50mph	18.4/– seconds	14.2/– seconds
Fuel consumption	30.6mpg (153 miles)	20-26mpg

Although inheriting the names Wyvern (4-cylinder) and Velox (6-cylinder), the new Vauxhall models announced in August 1951 were in most respects a considerable advance over the interim postwar models which bore these names.

As Vauxhall were pioneers of monocoque construction in Britain, it was no surprise that this method was chosen for the new bodyshell, and with the advantage of previous experience the Luton engineers were able to come up with a particularly roomy, yet extremely light construction. A notable feature was the swept down front inner wings with forward lower protrusions which were joined at the front by a single crossmember. As the front engine mountings and the independent suspension units were attached to this crossmember, a separate subframe with its associated extra weight was avoided. The front end design provided a roomy engine bay,

The elegant steering wheel and facia layout of LTM 815.

A bonnet which could be opened from either side, or removed altogether, was a feature of the early E-series models, but later gave way to a conventional rear-hinged arrangement.

access to which was made easy by an ingenious arrangement that allowed the bonnet to be opened from either side, or even be quickly removed altogether for total accessibility should this be necessary. With the absence of chassis type members, the roomy passenger compartment also utilised the front and rear bench seat mountings as transverse stiffeners for the lower regions. Entry was by four wide-opening front-hinged doors.

Directly over the rear axle line was a transversely mounted fuel tank with a useful 11 gallon capacity, and with the spare wheel being mounted under the boot floor, a large unobstructed luggage compartment was provided. A small access hole in the floor allowed the spare tyre pressure to be checked without having to lower and remove the wheel. The full width boot lid was counter-balanced, and came right down to the boot floor level, an arrangement which made for particularly easy loading: although the lack of a sill across the rear did rob the shell as a whole of some rigidity.

The overall length (14 feet 4 inches) and the wheelbase (8 feet 7 inches) were the same for both the four and six-cylinder cars, as were the chromium plated embellishments, leaving only the nameplates "Wyvern" or "Velox" to give any indication of which engine was installed. Being the products of a member of the mighty General Motors Corporation, the styling inevitably showed a transatlantic influence, although, apart from the rather heavy looking grille, the use of chromium was quite discreet. Although looking very up-to-date, a particularly neat touch was the way the stylists had incorporated the traditional Vauxhall "flutes" into the bonnet edges.

A large window area gave a light interior in which once again an American influence could be detected. The bench seats were upholstered in vynide, as were the door trims, both with a two colour finish on the Velox, the rear seat of which also featured a folding

A beautifully original 1953 Velox. The foglamp and wing mirrors are contemporary accessory items.

The rear window of the E-series Velox was of similar shape to the preceding model. LTM 815 was posing for the camera in 1984 – more than thirty years after leaving Luton.

centre armrest. Facing the driver was a graceful two spoked steering wheel, its plastic finish being either cream or black according to whether light or dark coloured upholstery was featured. The facia panel was a plastic moulding which housed two circular instruments immediately in front of the driver, one of which was the speedometer and mileage recorder with the other comprising a fuel gauge and engine temperature gauge. Swivelling quarter windows were provided in both front doors, but the main door windows were without winding mechanism, being of the balanced drop type which was a surprisingly cheap arrangement for this class of car.

The most unusual aspect of the mechanical specification was the continued use of the elderly long-stroked four and six-cylinder engines of the previous models, however, completely new units were at an advanced stage of development at Luton and would be phased into production early the following year. Of 1442cc and 2275cc the interim engines were of the overhead valve type, but developed a mere 35bhp and 54bhp respectively: figures which were hardly sufficient to provide the sort of performance that was expected from this type of car. The transmission consisted of a three-speed gearbox, with well-chosen ratios which were selected by a steering column lever. Synchronisation was provided between second and top gear, and the internals were almost wholly those of the previous models but now housed in a light alloy casing, a feature which gave a useful weight reduction. New hypoid rear axle assemblies with ratios of 4.625:1 (Wyvern), and 4.125:1 (Velox), gave sensibly high overall gearing of 16mph and 18.4mph per 1000rpm.

Although of conventional coil and wishbone design, the independent front suspension units were interesting in that the wishbones were fabricated from steel pressings rather than the usual forgings, and so here again there was a valuable weight reduction. The telescopic dampers were sealed units of Vauxhall's own design and manufacture. A Burman recirculating ball steering box ensured light control, and at 35 feet the turning circle was excellent in relation to the overall size of the car. The longitudinally mounted springs at the rear each consisted of only three leaves, but these were of very ample width at $2\frac{1}{4}$ inches. Lubrication between the leaves was incorporated during manufacture, and protected in use by gaiters around the springs both fore and aft of the axle.

The hydraulic braking system was developed in conjunction with the Lockheed company, and consisted of 9 inch diameter drums all round, which were cast integrally with the wheel hubs. The total lining area was $100\frac{1}{2}$ square inches. A pull-up handbrake lever was situated at the right-hand side of the driver's seat in such a position as to give excellent leverage. Five stud fixing was employed for the 15 inch diameter road wheels, these being shod with rather narrow section tyres, 5.60 and 5.90 for the Wyvern and Velox respectively.

In April 1952 the new short-stroked engines were introduced, thus giving the range a level of power and performance in keeping with their modern image. The bore and stroke measurements of 79.3 x 76.2mm gave cylinder capacities of 1508cc and 2262cc, figures which were particularly interesting in that they were identical in capacity and stroke/bore ratio to those decided upon by the Ford Motor Company two years previously for their Consul/Zephyr range. With 45bhp at 4000rpm and 71lbs/ft torque at 2000rpm to cope with an unladen weight of 20.8cwt, the Wyvern was now into the 70mph category, and could accelerate from rest to 60mph in 31 seconds. Accompanying this useful performance was the ability to cover more than 30 miles on one gallon of petrol when cruising at around 55mph, and an overall fuel consumption in the 27/28mpg bracket. Priced at £771, the Wyvern now offered particularly good value in the 1½-litre class, with an overall level of economy which could not quite be matched elsewhere amongst full six-seater cars.

With its new six-cylinder engine turning out 65bhp at 4000rpm and 108lbs/ft torque at the remarkably low engine speed of 1200rpm, the Velox was now both a lively and flexible performer. Accelerating from rest through the gears, 60 and 70mph could be reached in around 21 and 31 seconds respectively, on the way to a maximum which could just exceed a genuine 80mph. Equally

A 1954 advertisement highlights Wyvern and Velox virtues and Vauxhall value.

Spacious...Powerful...Economical

How brilliantly these two Vauxhalls meet the needs of motorists today. Velox and Wyvern alike are roomy, powerful, easily manœuvrable cars, a pleasure to drive and completely comfortable for five or even six passengers to ride in.

They are handsome and beautifully finished, yet at the same time surprisingly economical both in first cost and in petrol consumption. Higher compression "square" engines boost power, run longer without overhaul, and reduce petrol consumption. Expert and inexpensive maintenance is assured by Vauxhall Square Deal Service, operated by dealers in every part of the country with factory trained mechanics, immediately available parts and standard repair times.

For the owner who wants every penny of motoring value, these roomy, powerful, economical Vauxhalls are unequalled on the road today. Your Vauxhall dealer will be happy to arrange a demonstration run for you.

That's Vauxhall Value!

THE 6-CYLINDER VELOX
Maximum speed of 80 m.p.h. 28·68 m.p.g. at an average speed of 40·89 m.p.h ★ Spacious 5/6 seater. Length 14 ft. 4 ins., turning circle only 38 ft. Price £535 plus £224 . 0s. 10d. P.T.

THE 4-CYLINDER WYVERN
Same size body and the same modern styling as the Velox. Maximum speed of 70 m.p.h. 33·46 m.p.g. at an average speed of 30·51 m.p.h. ★ Price £495 plus £207 . 7s. 6d. P.T.

Vauxhall Motors Ltd · Luton · Beds.   ★ From R.A.C. observed petrol consumption tests.

important was the strong acceleration from below 20mph in the high top gear, enabling brisk progress to be accompanied by fuel consumption which was modest by six-cylinder standards, with an overall 24/25mpg being within easy reach. Handling qualities although not in the sports saloon class, but still appreciably more than just adequate for the Wyvern, were rather less so for the Velox, and the 100 square inches of brake lining area also seemed somewhat marginal for the 80mph car. However, taken as a whole, the Velox offered remarkable value at a price of £833, a figure which for a short time in fact made it the least expensive six-cylinder car available in Britain.

An improved facia panel was also phased in during 1952. Of similar design to the original, the panel was now formed as a metal pressing, and featured chrome plated bezels for the circular instrument housings. In June 1953 a conventional rear-hinged bonnet top replaced the earlier side opening arrangement, and in August of that year, Vauxhall distributors G.E. Neville & Son, of Mansfield, offered an overdrive conversion kit for both the four and six-cylinder cars. Priced at £58. 15s. 0d, which included a shortened propeller shaft on an exchange basis, plus £7. 10s. 0d. fitting charge, the overdrive was the well known Laycock de Normanville unit, and was controlled by a three position switch mounted on the gearlever. In the central position the overdrive was disengaged, in the upper position was engaged and under the driver's control. With the switch in the lower position the overdrive was engaged and disengaged automatically at predetermined speeds by a Lucas governor, cutting in at 42mph and dropping out at 36mph on the Wyvern; in and out at 36mph and 30mph on the Velox.

Early in 1954 a 7.3:1 compression ratio cylinder head was made available as a no cost option as an alternative to the standard 6.5:1 head. Necessitating the use of premium grade fuels, the 7.3:1 head resulted in a slight improvement in acceleration, and a small but useful improvement in the already notable fuel economy of these cars.

In October 1954, the range was extended with the introduction of the Cresta. Based on the Velox, the Cresta was in effect a De Luxe version of the six-cylinder model and was

The revised frontal treatment for 1955 shows up well on this preserved Wyvern. The rear wheelarch spats, wheeltrim rings and whitewall tyres were not standard equipment on the four-cylinder car.

recognizable externally by its two tone paint scheme and whitewall tyres in addition to its ''Cresta'' script. Standard equipment included a heater unit, which was of a new design, whilst the interior boasted two tone leather upholstery, and a redesigned facia panel which featured a recessed circular speedometer in front of the driver, and a matching recess on the opposite side to take the speaker when the optional radio was specified. This facia was suitable for both right and left-hand drive, and was being shared with the two cheaper models. Other detail modifications throughout the range consisted of chrome plated top piston rings, a simplified gearchange mechanism, a flexible coupling introduced between the steering column and steering box, flashing direction indicators in place of the previous semaphore type, and a larger diameter petrol filler orifice.

Visibly distinguishing the updated models was a rather less ''heavy'' frontal appearance, which was arrived at by the introduction of a slightly lower bonnet top and a new diecast full-width grille consisting of narrow vertical slats. Further recognition points on the six-cylinder cars were the provision of over-riders on the redesigned bumpers, raised chromium trims along the top of the front wings (which acted as useful width indicators for the driver) and rear wheelarch spats. Purchase tax reductions some months earlier had lowered prices generally, and at £702, £759, and £844, the Wyvern, Velox and Cresta range was competitively priced alongside its most obvious rivals, Ford's Consul (£666), Zephyr Six (£754), and Zephyr Zodiac (£851).

Never regarded as sporting saloons, only very few of these Vauxhalls ever competed in international rallies. However, although no major awards were collected, a most notable achievement was 7th place overall by a locally entered Velox in the tough East African Safari in 1955.

Vauxhall's own caption to this press release photograph reads: "With better brakes, tubeless tyres, much improved vision and dozens of new features, the 1956 Vauxhalls are vastly better cars than the models they replace. The Cresta is available in either single-colour or, as here, in '3-phase' dual-colour schemes''.

Continuing their established policy of steady development, Vauxhall announced several more worthwhile modifications in October 1955. Wider and deeper front and rear screens, of 12% and 60% greater area, which were accompanied by a larger rear view mirror, gave a considerable improvement in vision for all occupants. All three models now featured window winding mechanism and new door locks, whilst interior trim improvements included vinyl roof lining and an improved vinyl "carskin" upholstery in two tone colour schemes for the Wyvern and Velox. Both the six-cylinder cars gained armrest/doorpulls, and a windscreen washer was standardised on the Cresta. In an effort to improve the durability of the bodywork a thicker paint film was now employed, resulting in a better exterior finish and an improved appearance on inside surfaces such as door pillars, etc. A chrome plated pressing with slightly fewer slats now replaced the diecast metal grille.

New brake drums, of the same dimensions as before but now cast separately from the hubs, enabled brake lining inspection to be carried out more easily, whilst an alteration in the front/rear braking effort from 59%/41% to 64%/36% reduced the previous tendency of these models to lock their rear wheels rather early under hard braking. New gearbox bearings were claimed to be quieter in operation and have longer life. A slight price increase accompanied these improvements, the Wyvern now costing £723, the Velox £794 whilst £897 was now being asked for the Cresta.

Despite the fact that development of the replacement models was at an advanced stage late in 1956, further modifications were incorporated in the E-series cars which were displayed at Earls Court in October that year. Both the standard and optional compression ratios were raised, to 6.8:1 and 7.7:1 respectively, and the engines

A recently restored example of the 1956 Cresta.

Revised frontal treatment yet again, this time for the 1957 models. The lack of rear wheel spats quickly identifies this as the Wyvern.

A considerable increase in luggage carrying capacity was provided by the Grosvenor Carriage Company estate car conversion.

The late E-series Cresta, one of the models most sought-after by today's Vauxhall enthusiasts.

...the new car you'll enjoy is a Vauxhall!

Vauxhall Cresta, 6 cylinders

also benefited from the adoption of the new Zenith 34VN carburettor. Electrically operated windscreen wipers finally replaced the camshaft driven mechanical arrangement which Vauxhall had previously favoured. The main distinguishing features for these last of the line models were a new, simpler grille of horizontal bars, and a new, almost full-length chrome strip along each side of the car. The two tone finish on the Cresta was now confined to a "flash" of contrasting colour applied just above wheelarch level, a feature which gave a slightly longer look than before. In addition to the cars on the Vauxhall stand, two other interesting Velox models could be seen, both of these being estate car conversions. These were being shown by the Grosvenor Carriage Co. Ltd., and Martin Walter Ltd., the latter who were to become very well known for their "Dormobile" conversion of the Vauxhall/Bedford CA van.

The Wyvern was deleted early in 1957, being replaced by the smaller F-series Victor model, which itself received a strengthened and uprated version of the Wyvern's engine. The two six-cylinder cars however remained in production, and in June received the improved versions of the six-cylinder engine, and the all-synchromesh gearbox which were ultimately intended for the replacement PA models in October.

Datapanel: Vauxhall E-Series Wyvern/Velox/Cresta

	Wyvern	Velox/Cresta
Engine	4 cyl, ohv	6 cyl, ohv
Capacity	1508cc	2262cc
Bore	79.3mm	79.3mm
Stroke	76.2mm	76.2mm
Compression ratio	6.5:1 (7.3:1 optional)	6.5:1 (7.3:1 optional)
Max BHP	45 @ 4000rpm	65 @ 4000rpm
	47 with high compression	67 with high compression
Max torque	71lbs/ft @ 2000rpm	108lbs/ft @ 1200rpm
Gearing	16mph/1000rpm	18.4mph/1000rpm
Tyres	5.60 x 15	5.90 x 15
Kerb weight	20.8cwt	22.1cwt
Overall length	14ft 4 1/2in	14ft 4 1/2in
Overall width	5ft 7in	5ft 7in
Wheelbase	8ft 7in	8ft 7in

Performance

	"The Autocar" road tests 1952	"The Autocar" 1952
Max speed:		
Top gear	70.5mph (mean)	80mph (mean)
	71mph (best)	86mph (best)
2nd gear	53mph	60mph
1st gear	24mph	32mph
Acceleration:		
0-30mph	7.8 seconds	5.9 seconds
0-50mph	20.0 seconds	14.3 seconds
0-60mph	31.5 seconds	20.9 seconds
0-70mph	–	31.8 seconds
	Top gear/2nd gear	Top gear/2nd gear
20-40mph	11.7/8.4 seconds	9.3/6.2 seconds
30-50mph	13.4/12.4 seconds	10.1/8.2 seconds
40-60mph	18.3/– seconds	12.1/– seconds
50-70mph	–/– seconds	17.9/– seconds
Fuel consumption	27.8mpg (506 miles)	25.7mpg (1280 miles)

In a decision taken in 1955, Vauxhall decided to widen their range by producing two distinct models of differing sizes to replace their large E-Series rather than continue with just two engine options in the same bodyshell.

The new four-cylinder car, the Victor, appeared first, in March 1957 and was considerably smaller than the Wyvern it was replacing, being aimed directly at those motorists who wished for a comfortably roomy but compact four-seater model of good performance rather than the inexpensive but quite large six-seater four-cylinder models generally available.

The basis of the Victor was a four door bodyshell of monocoque construction and devoid of welded in stiffening members in its lower regions, relying instead on an indentation in the floorpan (which acted as a crossmember), the sills, and substantial centre pillars for satisfactory rigidity. Prior to painting, the floorpan was coated with a layer of baked on plastic. A large glass area was a notable feature, the "panoramic" windscreen which was already established in America making its first appearance on a British car. Although of a conventional, and in this particular application very convenient general layout, styling for its own sake had played an important part in the development of the Victor. Both the front and rear wings bulged outward at their lower edges to meet with similar forward protruding bulges at the extremities of the bumper bars. The low, and full-width grille housed the sidelights and was also styled to blend in with the bumper, whilst at the rear the sidelight surrounds appeared as vertical extensions of the bumper extremities. The front wings again bulged outwards above wheel arch level, at which point the Vauxhall flutes were now situated.

On the Victor Super, which was in effect a de-luxe edition, there was a bright metal finish to all the window surrounds, and the exhaust system tail pipe on this model terminated in the offside bulge in the bumper. The bonnet was self-supporting as was the bootlid which came down to almost bumper level, and when opened revealed a very large and conveniently shaped luggage compartment. The spare wheel was housed in an upright position in the offside; whilst beneath the floor was an 8 gallon fuel tank, its filler tube terminating inside the rear wing with access to the cap via a hinged flap in the outer wing panel.

Despite the intrusion into the front door space by the reversed slope windscreen pillars the doors still featured opening quarter windows. The windscreen pillars did however render access to the front compartment more difficult than is usually the case. Although very definitely a four-seater only, a bench seat was provided in the front. Both seats were devoid of armrests, even in the Super model. The Super did however feature armrest/doorpulls all round, a half horn ring on the steering wheel, twin sunvisors and door-switch-operated interior lighting. Two-speed electric windscreen wipers – surprisingly still of the arrangement which left a large unswept area in the centre – were a standard fitting on both models, but a heater was only available at extra cost in both cases.

A very transatlantic-looking facia faced the occupants, with a glovebox and parcel shelf ahead of the passenger whilst the driver viewed the speedometer, engine temperature gauge and fuel gauge through the upper half of the steering wheel. The mileage recorder mounted centrally in the instrument panel featured a magnifying lens

Top left and right. Unlike the conversions of earlier Vauxhall saloons, the Victor estate car was a purpose-built model from Luton.

Middle left. Strong transatlantic influence was evident in the styling of the early Victor. YWD 562 is an immaculate surviving example which was photographed recently.

The Victor estate car . . .

LOW AND BEHOLD the fresh new look of the future. Here's an eye-catching, dual purpose estate car, with crisp, low lines, unequalled visibility and superb road-holding. Here's four-figure elegance in a wonderfully practical car with all these features :—

FULL PANORAMIC VISION   FOUR-DOOR COMFORT

FOLD AWAY REAR SEAT   COUNTERBALANCED TAIL DOOR

SUPERBLY ENGINEERED ALL-STEEL INTEGRAL BODY

with heavy-duty rear axle, springs and tyres.

Change at will from a 4/5 seater with extra-large luggage capacity to a 2/3 seater with 5' 4" of flat-floored load space behind the driver. Ask your Vauxhall dealer for full details and for a demonstration.

Tail door, balanced by torsion springs, stays open without supports.

TOP VALUE FOR MONEY AT £620 PLUS £311.7.0d. P.T

With Victor performance, roadability and economy, plus the extra luxury features of the Victor Super model.

A period Vauxhall publicity shot highlights the Victor's styling. The exhaust system terminated in the offside rear bumper on this, the 'Super' model.

cover making it particularly easy to read. A two colour interior treatment was applied to both models, but only in a grey and black combination with a cream headlining on the basic car, whereas three interior choices were available on the Super.

Although of the same bore and stroke measurements as in the Wyvern, 79.4 x 76.2mm, the 1508cc engine was otherwise almost wholly new. A new cylinder block now terminated well below the crankshaft centre-line, and the cylinder head now featured equal length holding-down bolts. These changes resulted in a useful increase in the stiffness of the unit as a whole, and the Victor engine was destined to gain an enviable reputation for longevity by four-cylinder standards. Separate inlet ports and a corresponding four branch inlet manifold for the single Zenith carburettor, coupled with larger inlet valves, were responsible for an increase in power output with 55bhp at 4200rpm now being quoted. This was with the standard compression ratio of 7.8:1, a low compression – 6.8:1 – was also available as an option. A good torque output at low rpm had long been an excellent feature of Vauxhall engines, and the Victor unit produced at least 80lbs/ft all the way between 1200rpm and 3400rpm, actually peaking at a figure of 84lbs/ft at 2400rpm.

The $7\frac{1}{4}$ inch diameter clutch was now operated by a pendant pedal – as were the brakes – this arrangement making its first appearance on a Vauxhall. The three-speed gearbox was notable for the provision of synchromesh with which to assist in the engagement of bottom gear with the car on the move, thus removing one of the principal objections usually levelled at three speed boxes. Gear selection was by a steering column-mounted lever. An open propeller shaft and a hypoid bevel rear axle with a ratio of 4.125:1 completed the transmission. Overall gearing was a sensible 16.3mph per 1000rpm.

The independent front suspension units consisted of pressed steel wishbones, and coil springs which embraced Vauxhall's own designed and manufactured hydraulic dampers. An anti-roll bar was also fitted, and the complete suspension units were mounted to a crossmember which was attached to the body through rubber mountings. Burman recirculating ball steering gear was once again employed. The longitudinally mounted rear leaf springs each consisted of only three leaves, and displayed a reverse camber at normal loads. The Lockheed hydraulic braking system featured 8 inch diameter drums which were of composite cast iron and steel construction, and inside which were shoes giving a total lining area of 92 square inches. Road wheels of 13 inch diameter were another feature new to Vauxhall and were fitted with tyres of 5.60 section which, whilst perfectly adequate for the Victor's weight (20cwt), nevertheless looked somewhat small on this boldly styled car.

On the road, the new Vauxhall could attain 60mph from rest in 25 seconds whilst on its way to a maximum of 75mph. A comfortable cruising speed was 60 to 65mph, at which rate the Victor would still return 27/28mpg. Accompanying this was a good blend of ride and handling qualities which, rather surprisingly, seemed biased in favour of the latter, with the Victor quickly gaining a good reputation for its well mannered road behaviour. Priced at £728 and £758 for the basic and Super, respectively, the Victor was offering excellent value in the $1\frac{1}{2}$-litre category, although during its early days some criticism was levelled at the car in respect of standard of finish.

Hooded headlamp rims appeared in August 1957, and were followed by the addition of a Vauxhall medallion on the boot lid in October. Newtondrive two-pedal control was made available as an extra cost option at £25 in March 1958, at which time a factory-built Victor Estate car was also announced. Priced at £931, the estate was based on the Super saloon. The two rear passenger doors now featured squared up window framing, and the provision of very slim rear pillars on the estate car rear end structure maintained the excellent overall visibility for which the saloon was noted. The tailgate was fitted with a full-width window and was hinged at the top, in the open position giving access to a 45 cubic feet compartment if the rear seats were not in use. The rear seat cushion was arranged to tip forward, after which the squab – which featured a ribbed metal back to match the rear floor – could be folded flat. Mechanical changes to the estate car were confined to those appropriate to the increased loads possible, and included stiffer rear springs – now with five leaves and strengthened mounting points – larger, 5.90 section tyres, heavier section side tubes for the rear axle and larger hub bearings. The overall gearing was reduced to 15.1mph per 1000rpm by the adoption of a 4.625:1 final drive ratio.

The bold styling of the Victor apparently proved more popular in overseas markets than in Britain, with some 65% of production during 1957/58 going to export markets, the Victor in fact being Britain's most exported car during that period. However, in an effort to improve home market sales a cleaned-up Mk2 model was introduced in February 1959. Still unmistakably a Victor, the Mk2 model nevertheless featured quite extensively re-worked outer panelling. The wings lost their bulbous lower regions, and the extremities of the car were now protected by conventional, and rather plain bumper bars. Smoother rear door skins were without the deep swage line of the earlier cars, and a simpler bonnet pressing now just had one stiffening rib. Elliptical sidelights were now incorporated in the extremities of the grille, the slight peak in the roof above the windscreen disappeared whilst at the rear, the boot lid was now without the swage line around the number plate. On the basic model, much of the previous bright metal was now painted to match the body colour, with the window frames and even the Vauxhall flutes receiving this treatment.

The range was however extended, with a new De-Luxe model being added above the Victor Super. The De-Luxe Victor was identified externally by the addition of a chrome strip extending from the flute to the rear of the car, with an appropriate additional piece of strip just ahead of the flute adjacent to the headlamp rim. This treatment formed the dividing line for new two-tone paint finishes which were being offered, and which in fact were also to be available on the Victor Super for an extra charge of £15. Wheeltrim rings and special hubcaps were further De-Luxe model features. Inside, separate front seats immediately identified the De-Luxe Victor, with these and the rear seat being upholstered in dual tone leather rather than the vynide of the two cheaper cars. More elaborate door trims and carpet underlay were other De-Luxe features, but the heater was still to remain an option. The bench front seat of the cheaper cars was re-designed to give more shoulder support, and, like the new separate seats in the De-Luxe, could now be adjusted for both height and rake by either removing or adding spacers at the front and rear mountings.

The rather more restrained styling of the MkII models shows up well in these recent photographs of an excellent surviving example.

4341 VX

4341 VX

Improved door sealing was introduced, and the floorpan now had a coating of a bituminous compound.

Mechanical changes were few, the Victor having already gained an excellent reputation in this respect, but changes to the cooling system were introduced. A larger fan pulley reduced fan speed and usefully cut down fan noise. The reduction in speed was compensated for by an increase in the fan diameter of 2 inches, and the fan was now drawing air through a slightly larger capacity radiator which was mounted lower than before. Improved production methods were said to have raised the overall quality of the Victor by a marked degree, and with prices of £758, £796 and £848 for the basic model, the Super and the De-Luxe, respectively, the Victor Mk2 was continuing to offer very good value. The estate car was actually now down in price to an attractive £908.

The bodywork was proving rather susceptible to corrosion, and in an effort to combat this the bituminous undersealing was extended to cover all the undersurfaces from October 1959, and splash shields to protect the inside of the finned rear wings were introduced in December. A further face-lift appeared in August 1960. At the front, the mesh grille was replaced by one of five horizontal bars, and now featured a badge in the centre. Above the grille, the word "VAUXHALL" now appeared along the bonnet front, and the headlamp hoods received a polished metal capping. A much deeper rear window was an instant recognition feature from behind; and the rear pillars were unadorned for the first time. Vertical flutes now appeared on the lower part of the boot lid, and a new catch enabled the boot to be opened without the use of the key if desired. A completely re-designed facia panel, with a padded top on the Super and De-Luxe cars, included a new speedometer with a horizontal scale. The switchgear, and heater controls when fitted, were now grouped more conveniently ahead of the driver, and, where applicable, there was a full horn ring. Apart from the adoption of copper-lead big end bearings, the mechanical specification remained as before, and the Victor continued in this configuration until replaced late in 1961 by the completely re-styled FB models.

Further cleaning-up of the styling came in October 1960. Pictured here in the Cotswolds is the top-of-the-line Victor de Luxe.

Datapanel: Vauxhall Victor F Series

Vauxhall Victor F Series

Engine	4 cyl, ohv
Capacity	1508cc
Bore	79.3mm
Stroke	76.2mm
Compression ratio	7.8:1
Max BHP	55 @ 4200rpm
Max torque	84lbs/ft @ 2400rpm
Gearing	16.3mph/1000rpm
Tyres	5.60 x 13
Kerb weight	20cwt
Overall length	14ft 0 1/2in
Overall width	5ft 3 3/4in
Wheelbase	8ft 2in

Performance

"The Motor"
R/T No. 7/59

Max speed:	
Top gear	75.3mph (mean)
	78.2mph (best)
2nd gear	52mph
1st gear	28mph
Acceleration:	
0-30mph	5.9 seconds
0-50mph	16.0 seconds
0-60mph	24.8 seconds
0-70mph	40.6 seconds
	Top gear/2nd gear
20-40mph	10.1/6.6 seconds
30-50mph	12.6/8.9 seconds
40-60mph	16.3/– seconds
50-70mph	22.9/– seconds
Fuel consumption	26.3mpg (1306 miles)

Whereas the styling of the Victor had been received with mixed feelings, that of the new PA series Velox and Cresta models received almost unanimous approval on the model's introduction in October 1957, and, more than 25 years later, the PA is still regarded by many Vauxhall enthusiasts as the best looking car ever to leave the Luton factory.

Greater in length and width by 5 inches and 2 inches, respectively, over the previous model, and lower by 4 1/2 inches, the new bodyshell offered generous accommodation for six people and their luggage. Headroom remained the same as before thanks to a low floor line achieved partly by sloping the engine/gearbox combination down slightly towards the rear in conjunction with a forward tilt to the nosepiece of the rear axle, thus lowering the height of the propelle shaft. The bodyshell was notable in that apart from the hinged panels (the four doors, boot and bonnet top), all the panels were stress bearing to some degree. As a result of this, in glazed condition the larger body was only 50lbs or so heavier than its predecessors. Box section pillars, and two horizontal ribs along the roof – these continuing down to the rear deck, and thus forming part of the divisions for the three piece rear window – played their part in the overall rigidity. The panoramic windscreen, too, was said to be making a useful contribution to the stiffness of the structure as a whole. Aiding stiffness in the lower regions were box section members running along each side of the car and two crossmembers: that at the front being to take the independent front suspension units, and the one at the rear forming the forward mounting points for the longitudinal leaf springs. Apart from the front wings, all the undersurfaces were coated with a plastic material.

With the wide front doors, the panoramic windscreen intruded rather less than on the Victor, making entry to the front compartment rather easier on these big Vauxhalls. The spring loaded bonnet was very wide, terminating in fact along what would normally be the top centre line of the front wings. At the rear, the bootlid came down almost to bumper level: counterbalanced, it opened to reveal a very large and conveniently-shaped luggage compartment. The spare wheel was housed in a recess in the flat floor, and was complete with a circular cover plate. A 10 1/2 gallon fuel tank resided behind the rear seat squab hidden from view in the boot behind a false back panel, and with its filler cap beneath a flap on the nearside of the flat rear deck.

Bright metal embellishments were a prominent external feature, the chrome plated grille including extensions at each end housing separate side and direction indicator lights. Chrome also surrounded the headlights, and a similar strip finished off the front edge of the bonnet top. A substantial looking bumper at the front had its centre section lower than its two extremities, thus cleverly avoiding the need for separate over-riders. The outer sections also curved round to offer useful front wing corner protection. In contrast, the rear bumper, which was styled at its ends to encompass the lower part of the large oval sidelights, looked rather more decorative than useful. A broad horizontal strip ran from the front of the car just above wheel arch level; narrowing gradually to a point at the rear. Concave throughout almost its entire length, this strip represented the traditional Vauxhall flutes. The door window frames, and the screen surrounds were of stainless steel, polished on the Cresta but painted

The distinctive tail-end styling is shown off perfectly in this recent view of a well-preserved and very original 1958 Velox.

An early PA Cresta photographed from a most impressive viewpoint – it was undoubtedly a stylish car.

Glittering unashamedly, epitomising the 1950s, this PA Cresta poses before the camera some 25 years or so after leaving the Luton factory.

over in the body colour on the less expensive Velox. The Cresta could be further identified by a bonnet motif, special wheel discs, whitewall tyres and an optional two-tone paint scheme which, when specified, featured the second colour on the roof and rear deck only.

Standard equipment included twin sunvisors, twin two-speed electric wipers, twin horns, armrests on all four doors and a rear folding centre armrest. Additionally, on the Cresta, were an electric clock, windscreen washers, glovebox lamp, cigar lighter, vanity mirror and heater. Two shrouded circular dials faced the driver, one being the speedometer and the other housing the ammeter, and gauges for engine temperature and fuel contents level. A two-spoked steering wheel was fitted, and featured a half horn ring on the Cresta. Both the bench seats were upholstered in vynide on the Velox, whereas on the Cresta the buyer had a choice of leather, rayon, or elastofab, each with a dual tone finish. The Cresta door trims too were finished in dual tones.

The mechanical specification was identical in both models. The engine was in effect a six-cylinder version of the uprated Victor unit, featuring a deep skirt block and cylinder head with separate ports. This unit had appeared four months earlier in the last of the E-series Velox/Cresta models, and the only difference now in the PA installation was the adoption of a newer Zenith carburettor incorporating an automatic choke controlled by a thermostat in the exhaust manifold. On the standard compression ratio of 7.8:1 – 6.8:1 being optional for those who wished to use low grade fuel – 76bhp was developed at 4400rpm, this being accompanied by 124lbs/ft

A conveniently-shaped load area with unrestricted access was a good feature of the Friary estate.

torque at 1800rpm. The steering column lever-controlled three-speed gearbox was now fully synchronised, and was transmitting the power to the rear wheels via a new rear axle assembly with a ratio of 4.11:1. The crownwheel was of larger diameter than before, and heavier duty differential bearings were used. Overall gearing was now 17.5mph per 1000rpm.

The running gear followed the recent Vauxhall practice, with pressed steel wishbones and coil springs forming the independent front suspension units. An anti-roll bar was incorporated at the front and the steering gear was once again of the recirculating ball type. The longitudinally mounted rear springs had a slight reverse camber, and each consisted of four 2 1/4 inch wide leaves. The Lockheed hydraulic brakes were now operated by a pendant pedal – as was the hydraulic clutch – and the drums were housing shoes with 137 square inches of lining area. New 13 inch diameter roadwheels were fitted with 6.40 section tyres.

Introduced at prices of £983 and £1073, the Velox and Cresta were in direct competition with Dagenham's Mk2 Zephyr (£916) and Zodiac (£1013), and were offering broadly similar performance, economy, accommodation and equipment. A maximum speed of almost exactly 90mph was accompanied by a rate of acceleration which would allow 70mph to be reached from rest in about 25/26 seconds. Rather heavier – at 23½cwt – than the preceding E-series, and with lower overall gearing, fuel consumption had suffered slightly with an overall figure now in the 22/23mpg bracket.

A very attractive combination of practicality and style, the Friary estate conversion.

Several small, but worthwhile improvements were phased into production during the latter half of 1958, heavier gauge steel for the bonnet top reduced the tendency of this panel to flex when the car was being driven over poorly surfaced roads. Wider front quarter windows gave improved visibility and, thanks to a new manufacturing process, there was less distortion through the corner pieces of the three piece rear window. On the Cresta there was now a folding centre armrest for the front seat occupants, a new woven nylon covering as a further upholstery option, and the application of sound deadening material beneath the rear parcel shelf.

An estate car conversion became available in May 1959, with the necessary work being carried out by Friary Motors Ltd., of Basingstoke. A full-width top hinged tailgate, complete with a self-supporting strut, gave access to the luggage space, the flat floor and sides of which were covered in black vinyl. The back of the rear seat squab too, was similarly covered, and now featured a lipped top edge which would prevent spillage when the squab was folded flat. Beneath the wide flat floor was a circular recess of sufficient depth to house two spare wheels, although only one was provided. Surrounding this well, with straight outer and end walls and semi-circular inside walls were twin fuel tanks giving a total capacity of 14 gallons. Both tanks were filled via the same orifice in the nearside rear wing. The extended roof of the Estate resulted in 1 1/2 inches extra headroom for rear seat passengers, and the additional rear side windows sloped backwards to match the rear passenger door window frames. An offside wing mirror was a standard feature, and the overall result was a particularly stylish estate car model. 6 ply tyres and an additional leaf in each rear spring were the only technical changes, and both Velox and Cresta versions were available at £1222 and £1308, respectively. Owners of existing saloons could have the work carried out by Friary Motors at a cost of £283, but this did not include the heavy duty springs and tyres.

Purchase tax reductions lowered the saloon prices to £929 and £1014, and the range continued unchanged until August 1959 at which time facelifted models were announced. A single piece rear window now replaced the earlier arrangement, and was in conjunction with a new roof panel without the stiffening ribs. Rigidity was restored however by structural modifications to the rear door pillars and the parcel shelf area. At the front was a new grille with a raised centre section, and along the sides was a thin chromium strip replacing the earlier broad concave embellishment – the Vauxhall flutes had finally disappeared. The new side strips were also now the division for the Cresta's two-tone paint finish, with the lower half colour also now being applied to the roof; thus giving a sandwich effect. Inside, redesigned seats were said to give more comfort, and thanks to the repositioning of the fuel tank slightly further rearwards the rear seat was now placed 1 inch further back, improving knee room by that amount. The Cresta's horn ring was now a full circle, and the standard heater unit – still only an option on the Velox – was of a new Smith's design. Under the bonnet was a larger radiator and a shroud for the cooling fan to assist engine cooling in hot climatic conditions.

Major improvements, including a new, larger capacity engine were announced in August 1960. A new cylinder block, with bores of 82.55mm and more widely spaced than before, was 2 1/4 inches

Marvellous new cars

these 1960 Vauxhalls

New Vauxhall 'Sixes'
Velox £655 + £274.0.10. PT (£929.0.10)
Cresta (illustrated) £715 + £299.0.10. PT (£1014.0.10)

longer, and permitted the use of a crankshaft with longer bearing journals. The revised crankshaft throw now gave a stroke also of 82.55mm, thus giving the new unit a capacity of 2651cc. Larger valves opened into wedge shaped combustion chambers in a new cylinder head which gave a compression ratio of 8.0:1. A single Zenith carburettor was retained, and the engine output figures were now 95bhp at 4600rpm and 138lbs/ft torque at 1600rpm. A larger diameter clutch was fitted, but the gearbox remained unchanged. A new rear axle ratio of 3.9:1 in conjunction with 14 inch road wheels and 5.90 section tyres raised the overall gearing to 18.8mph per 1000rpm. The increased diameter wheels were in fact chosen to allow larger brake drums, those at the front now being 10 inches in diameter whilst the rears remained unchanged at 9 inches. Vacuum servo assistance was available at extra cost.

The rectangular sidelights, and the extension of the roof colour to include the fins, are further 2.6-litre model identification features.

The headlamps were now Lucas sealed beam units, and restyled sidelight/direction indicator light treatment both front and rear, with a plainer but more substantial looking rear bumper were external features which identified these latest models. The hubcaps were also restyled, and the Cresta was now sporting new anodised aluminium wheel trims with elongated brake cooling slats. Facing the occupants was a new full width padded facia top incorporating a new horizontal speedometer ahead of the driver. A revolving drum behind the speedometer face was coloured so that green appeared on the scale up to 30mph, amber between 30 and 60mph, and red thereafter. The prices of both cars remained unchanged, and a Laycock-de Normanville overdrive was now available as an option for an extra £64.

Automatic transmission became available two months later – at an extra cost of £170 – the system chosen being a developed version of the General Motors Hydra-Matic transmission which dated back to 1939. This latest automatic gearbox had been developed by General Motors for their new generation of "compact" cars in America, and with its three forward speeds and torque multiplication on low gear only, it absorbed rather less engine power than other types and was therefore well suited to European cars in the 2 1/2-litre category.

Servo assisted disc brakes became an optional extra in October 1961, at which time separate front seats could also be specified. The Velox acquired a horn ring, and wood trim was incorporated in the facia and door cappings on the luxury Cresta. The PA series continued in production for a further year until replaced by the completely rebodied, and larger, PB series.

Redesigned tail lights and rear bumper were external identification features of the 2.6-litre-engined cars. Here a Cresta is running at speed over a ripple road test track.

Datapanel: Vauxhall Velox/Cresta PA Series

	Vauxhall Velox 2.3-litre	Cresta PA 2.6-litre
Engine	6 cyl, ohv	6 cyl, ohv
Capacity	2262cc	2651cc
Bore	79.3mm	82.55mm
Stroke	76.2mm	82.55mm
Compression ratio	7.8:1	8.1:1
Max BHP	76 @ 4400rpm	95 @ 4600rpm
Max torque	124lbs/ft @ 1800rpm	138lbs/ft @ 1600rpm
Gearing	17.5mph/1000rpm	18.8mph/1000rpm
Tyres	6.40 x 13	5.90 x 14
Kerb weight	23 1/2cwt	22 3/4cwt
Overall length	14ft 10in	15ft
Overall width	5ft 8 1/2in	5ft 8 1/2in
Wheelbase	8ft 9in	8ft 9in

Performance

	"The Motor" R/T No. 24/59 2.3 litre Estate Car	"The Motor" R/T No. 6/62/
Max speed:		
Top gear	88.7mph (mean)	93.3mph (mean)
	90.0mph (best)	96.8mph (best)
2nd gear	60mph	62mph
1st gear	37mph	35mph
Acceleration:		
0-30mph	4.7 seconds	4.8 seconds
0-50mph	11.6 seconds	11.5 seconds
0-60mph	17.6 seconds	16.3 seconds
0-70mph	26.1 seconds	22.5 seconds
0-80mph	40.6 seconds	31.0 seconds
	Top gear/2nd gear	Top gear/2nd gear
20-40mph	9.5/5.6 seconds	9.4/5.8 seconds
30-50mph	10.2/6.7 seconds	9.5/6.2 seconds
40-60mph	10.7/– seconds	10.8/– seconds
50-70mph	14.0/– seconds	11.9/– seconds
60-80mph	23.0/– seconds	14.5/– seconds
Fuel consumption	21.8mpg (1212 miles)	21.6mpg (3532 miles)

Chapter 8

An Enthusiast's Guide

Thirty years on, the fifties family saloon can offer the car enthusiast an inexpensive way of running something that is so obviously different from the crowd at a time when, due to its fuel-saving wind tunnel-inspired shape the modern car is becoming ever more difficult to identify individually: each new model seeming to be a little more anonymous than its predecessor.

In contrast, despite the temporary upset to oil supplies caused by the closure of the Suez Canal in 1956, fuel consumption figures somehow never seemed to be of vital importance in the 1950s, whereas styling for its own sake was an important aspect which, in the opinion of many people, resulted in some of Britain's most handsome cars making their appearance in that early postwar period.

Since the middle 1970s, interest has grown in these cars to such an extent that there now exists a network of thriving owners' clubs and spares specialists catering specifically for these models. These organisations, by pooling their knowledge, locating spares and in some cases arranging the remanufacture of unobtainable spares items, have now removed many of the problems which the casual observer might think would make it difficult to run a twenty or thirty-year-old car on an everyday basis. Some models are inevitably better placed than others in respect of spares availability, and therefore more suitable than the others as everyday transport, with the BMC (Austin/Morris) and Ford products seeming to be the best catered for in so far as regular service items and major mechanical components are concerned.

Although the cars themselves are obviously no longer in plentiful supply, examples of all the models under review do nevertheless crop up for sale from time to time, and the open-minded enthusiast with no particular favourite should find it relatively easy to get into the current fifties motoring scene. Asking prices vary widely, but there is certainly no need to pay "over the odds", and as a general rule a tidy and solid example of any fifties family model can be purchased at a price which would put it well down towards the lower end of the current used car market.

All of these cars are now recognised as being "collectible", and those which were at the very economy end of the new car market are perhaps better viewed as a collectors' car or at least as a second car which will be used for pleasure only. The performance of these small models, the A30, Morris Minor MM or series II, Standard Eight and the "upright" Fords is such that whilst they can perhaps maintain adequate progress from the point of view of the journey itself, they certainly cannot hope to live with the traffic stream under many conditions which are encountered today, and particularly so when all four seats are occupied. The slightly more powerful versions of these cars, the A35, Minor 1000 and Standard Ten will fare rather better: the increase in torque from their larger engines being perhaps more useful than the improved top-end power. In overall performance the 100E Ford is a good match for these, although the rather wide gap between its second and top gear ratios seems rather more noticeable in today's conditions than was the case in the model's heyday. So, the old car enthusiast who still likes to "get his foot down" from time to time may well find the relative lack of power from these small cars a little frustrating at times. However, if the modest performance is not considered to be a drawback, then any of these economy cars can still give a lot of pleasure today, and, usually, at very modest cost indeed.

Moving up the scale slightly there are the compact but quite roomy models which also offered rather more performance than the very small cars. The Austin A40s, Hillman Minx, and later the Vauxhall Victor were popular examples of this class of car. In terms of performance today, the sidevalve Minx and the Austin Devon/Somerset series are well down the league, but should still prove capable of maintaining adequate progress. Both the ohv Minx and the Victor have quite lively acceleration, and should be attractive to the enthusiast who wants a comfortably roomy four-seater allied to a 75mph capability. Of these two, the Minx seems to be rather more available, whilst the Victor, which did prove to be somewhat more rust prone than most is now a comparative rarity amongst fifties cars.

Any of the popular $1\frac{1}{2}$-litre medium/large models, the A50/55 Cambridge, MkI Consul, Vauxhall Wyvern and the Morris Oxfords will offer pleasurable motoring today. The sidevalve Oxford however will not match the others in performance, and is in any case now very rare. All the Oxfords were very well trimmed for this class of car, and a Series II/III in good condition should be a tempting proposition for the enthusiast who wants an acceptable performance allied to a well appointed and roomy interior. The Oxford also offers quite good handling qualities, being bettered only by the Consul in this class. Both the Consul and the Cambridge are rather more compact than the Oxford, thus offering slightly less room, and neither are quite so well appointed. They are generally a little quicker however, and the Consul particularly is still quite widely available. The Wyvern offers more room than all the others in the $1\frac{1}{2}$-litre category and its larger bodywork is no heavier than its smaller rivals; as it is pulling higher overall gearing than these it should usually prove more economical at open-road cruising speeds. In sheer speed and acceleration however, it will not quite match the rest of this class.

Offering appreciably more room than average in the under 2-litre category is the Consul Mk2. Its 1703cc engine more than compensates for the small weight increase imposed by the larger body and also enables it to pull higher gearing than the typical $1\frac{1}{2}$-litre models; also, of all the inexpensive 4-cylinder cars, it is perhaps the happiest at motorway speeds.With the middle ratio of its three-speed gearbox being useful up around 50mph, the Consul can also maintain its position quite well in modern traffic. Built in large quantities, it has survived very well; its availability today making it a quick and easy way for the enthusiast to buy into the fifties scene.

In terms of performance and accommodation the 1670cc Standard Ensign closely matches the Consul, but unfortunately this model saw only limited production and therefore is a rarity today. Nevertheless, a good example would no doubt offer pleasurable motoring; its scarcity value also making it somewhat more "collectable" than the rival Ford.

Before leaving the smaller/medium engined models, it is perhaps worth pointing out that by comparison with similar sized-engines in today's cars, these units all develop their peak torque and bhp outputs at much lower rpm. This results in a level of smooth low-speed flexibility in top gear almost unknown in modern cars of similar capacity, thus making these older models feel rather more effortless than their modest acceleration and maximum speed figures might suggest.

Those enthusiasts who insist on a rapid overtaking performance, easy top gear hill-climbing and cruising near the legal limit on the motorway, should always choose from the over 2-litre category. Sadly, very few of the early postwar examples now remain, most having disappeared before the recent upsurge in interest in the period. Nevertheless, a good example of a Morris Six, Vanguard Phase I/II or an Austin A70 would certainly give much more than just adequate performance for today's conditions, although the rarity value of these is such that they are really better thought of as collectable, rather than day-in day-out usable Classics.

With the MkI Zephyr, Ford brought high-performance six-cylinder motoring within the reach of many people for the first time, although Vauxhall quickly followed with their E-series Velox, actually undercutting the Zephyr's price for a short time in 1952. Plenty of good examples of the MkI Zephyr and its luxury companion, the Zephyr Zodiac, have survived, and are quite at home in modern conditions where their outstanding top gear flexibility in particular still makes them brisk and effortless performers in today's traffic. Top gear is however a little on the low side, and although the short-stroke unit never complains about holding high rpm, the 70mph motorway cruise does sound a little busy. Good handling qualities accompany the Zephyr's lively performance.

The enthusiast wishing for a little more room than this rather compact Ford may well find that the E-series Velox is just what is wanted. Roomier than the MkI Zephyr by a useful margin, and just as quick in a straight line, the Velox and its fully equipped companion model Cresta are in fact also lighter in weight. This enables them to pull rather higher gearing which gives them a worthwhile advantage over the Zephyr in touring fuel consumption and a more relaxed motorway cruise. Unfortunately, relatively few of these elegant Vauxhalls seem to have survived, but if this model does fit the bill, then it should be worth looking hard to find the right example.

The early Westminster will also more than hold its own on the road today, whilst the later A95, and particularly the higher-powered and fully equipped A105 would seem to be a very attractive proposition indeed. Unfortunately, the Westminster's BMC stablemate, the Morris Isis, sold only in small numbers, and finding a good example of this model today could be a lengthy task. Also a rapid performer, particularly so in their later 2.6-litre form, are Vauxhall's PA Velox/Cresta. Of all the models under review however, these appear to have been the least rust resistant by a considerable margin; this factor more than anything else being responsible for their scarcity today. Bearing this in mind, a well preserved or restored PA would really be better thought of as a collectors' item, and therefore not be subjected to the rigours of everyday, or wet weather motoring.

Rather slower in a straight line than either the Austin A105 or the 2.6-litre PA Vauxhall, the Mk2 Zephyr/Zodiac is nevertheless a very lively and effortless car, and as with the earlier Zephyrs, good handling qualities are another strong point. Built in greater numbers than its rivals, it has also enjoyed a good survival rate, and as a result is the easiest way for the enthusiast to go fifties-style six-cylinder motoring. Also in this sector were the Phase III and Vignale Vanguards, the quickest of which, the Sportsman, was built only over a very short period of time. However, the more numerous lower output models, whilst not matching the acceleration of their larger engined six-cylinder rivals, should still cope well enough on the road today.

Locating examples of these cars which are for sale is usually easy enough, several excellent monthly magazines devoted to older cars of many types are now in circulation and the classified columns of these usually contain a small selection of fifties family models. Whatever the final choice, the new owner should waste no time in joining the appropriate owners' club and, if possible, should make an effort to attend the meetings which are arranged. Much useful information and advice is freely swapped amongst the membership of these clubs, and the friendships formed can add quite considerably to the pleasures of fifties family motoring – thirty years on.

Appendix
Owners' Clubs

Austin A30-A35 Owners' Club. SAE to 42 Boswell Road, Doncaster DN4 7DD

Austin Cambridge/Westminster Car Club. SAE to 2 Bloomfield Close, Timsbury, Bath

Austin Counties Car Club. SAE to 68 Upper Road, Plaistow, London E13 0DH

Ford Sidevalve Owners' Club. SAE to 24 Kellett Grove, Leeds LS12

Ford MkI Consul/Zephyr/Zodiac Owners' Club. SAE to 8 Park Farm Close, Shadoxhurst, Nr. Ashford, Kent TN26 1LD

Ford Mk2 Consul/Zephyr/Zodiac Owners' Club. SAE to 170 Conisborough Crescent, Catford, London SE6

Hillman Owners' Club. SAE to 39 Barton Drive, Bradley Barton, Newton Abbot, Devon

Morris Minor Owners' Club. SAE to 127-129 Green Lane, Derby DE1 1RZ

Morris Oxford MO & 6/80 Club. SAE to 67 Fleetgate, Barton-on-Humber, North Lincs DN18 5QD

Morris Cowley/Oxford Club. SAE to 28 Dermott Avenue, Comber, Co. Down BT23 5JE

Standard Motor Club. SAE to Flat 1, 52 Selbourne Road, Southgate, London N14 7DH

Vauxhall Owners' Club (pre 1957). SAE to 19 South Road, Portishead, Bristol BS20 9DU

Vauxhall PA Owners' Club. SAE to 39 Kent Gardens, Ealing, London W13 8BU

The F Victor Owners' Club. SAE to 65 Huntingdon Close, Mitcham, Surrey